A Letter from Carrie Pickett:

We are excited to invite you on a journey where time management is not about just fitting more into your day, but how you let God manage your days so you fulfill His plans and purposes for your life!

Our desire in creating this system was so you can learn to be intentional and strategic with the goals and vision God created you to fulfill. You were created to accomplish great things through your relationship with God!

Proverbs 9:6, 11 - "Leave your simple ways, and live and walk in the way of insight. For by me your days will be multiplied, and years will be added to your life."

So dream big and surrender this day to the Lord! Rejoice and be glad in it!

Carrie V. Pickett

Assistant VP of Charis Bible College
Director of Global Training

> Gaurd well your spare moments. They are like uncut diamonds. Discard them and their value will never be known. Improve them and they will become the brightest gems in a useful life.
> - *Ralph Waldo Emerson*

If found, please return to :

_____

_____

Email : _____

Phone : _____

Year : _____

Quarter : _____

To watch the *tutorial vidoes* for the Intentional Planner, please log on to the web address below through your web browser.

www.intentional-planner.com

Contents

My Annual Goals	1
Achievement Goal Templates	2
Habit Goal Templates	8
Daily Rituals	14
Monthly Calendar	
Month 1	13
Month 2	108
Month 3	200
Brain Storming Pages	292
Study Subject Pages	304
Books to Buy Pages	312
Note Pages	316
Additional Monthly Calendars	356
Reading Plan	362

My Goals for the Year

Write your goals here and review them daily.
What will it take to make this year your best year?

1.

2.

3.

4.

5.

6.

7.

8.

9.

* Use an astrick to mark those goals you want to focus on this trimester.

Write your Achievement Goal

☐ Q1 ☐ Q2 ☐ Q3 ☐ Q4   Deadline _____

Domain of Life this will affect:
☐ SPIRITUAL   ☐ PARENTAL
☐ MARITAL   ☐ PHYSICAL   ☐ INTELLECTUAL   ☐ VOCATIONAL
☐ SOCIAL   ☐ FINANCIAL   ☐ AVOCATIONAL   ☐ EMOTIONAL

_____
_____
_____
_____
_____

My Top 3 Motivations

The Reward
How will you celebrate the achievement of your Goal!

My first 3 Steps

Additional Goal Steps:

Write your Achievement Goal

☐ Q1 ☐ Q2 ☐ Q3 ☐ Q4   Deadline _____

Domain of Life this will affect:
☐ MARITAL   ☐ PHYSICAL   ☐ SPIRITUAL   ☐ PARENTAL
☐ SOCIAL   ☐ FINANCIAL   ☐ INTELLECTUAL   ☐ VOCATIONAL
                               ☐ AVOCATIONAL   ☐ EMOTIONAL

_____
_____
_____
_____
_____

My Top 3 Motivations

The Reward
How will you celebrate the achievement of your Goal!

My first 3 Steps

Additional Goal Steps:

Write your Achievement Goal

☐ Q1 ☐ Q2 ☐ Q3 ☐ Q4   Deadline _____

Domain of Life this will affect:
☐ SPIRITUAL   ☐ PARENTAL
☐ MARITAL   ☐ PHYSICAL   ☐ INTELLECTUAL   ☐ VOCATIONAL
☐ SOCIAL   ☐ FINANCIAL   ☐ AVOCATIONAL   ☐ EMOTIONAL

_____
_____
_____
_____
_____

My Top 3 Motivations

The Reward
How will you celebrate the achievement of your Goal!

My first 3 Steps

Additional Goal Steps:

Write your Achievement Goal

☐ Q1 ☐ Q2 ☐ Q3 ☐ Q4   Deadline _____

Domain of Life this will affect:
- ☐ SPIRITUAL
- ☐ PARENTAL
- ☐ MARITAL
- ☐ PHYSICAL
- ☐ INTELLECTUAL
- ☐ VOCATIONAL
- ☐ SOCIAL
- ☐ FINANCIAL
- ☐ AVOCATIONAL
- ☐ EMOTIONAL

My Top 3 Motivations

The Reward
How will you celebrate the achievement of your Goal!

My first 3 Steps

Additional Goal Steps:

Write your Achievement Goal

☐ Q1 ☐ Q2 ☐ Q3 ☐ Q4   Deadline _____

Domain of Life this will affect:
☐ SPIRITUAL ☐ PARENTAL
☐ MARITAL ☐ PHYSICAL ☐ INTELLECTUAL ☐ VOCATIONAL
☐ SOCIAL ☐ FINANCIAL ☐ AVOCATIONAL ☐ EMOTIONAL

_____
_____
_____
_____
_____

My Top 3 Motivations

The Reward
How will you celebrate the achievement of your Goal!

My first 3 Steps

Additional Goal Steps:

Write your Achievement Goal

☐ Q1 ☐ Q2 ☐ Q3 ☐ Q4   Deadline _____

Domain of Life this will affect: ☐ SPIRITUAL   ☐ PARENTAL
☐ MARITAL   ☐ PHYSICAL   ☐ INTELLECTUAL   ☐ VOCATIONAL
☐ SOCIAL   ☐ FINANCIAL   ☐ AVOCATIONAL   ☐ EMOTIONAL

My Top 3 Motivations

The Reward
How will you celebrate the achievement of your Goal!

My first 3 Steps

Additional Goal Steps:

Write your Habit Goal

☐ Q1 ☐ Q2 ☐ Q3 ☐ Q4   Deadline _____

Domain of Life this will affect: ☐ SPIRITUAL   ☐ PARENTAL
☐ MARITAL   ☐ PHYSICAL   ☐ INTELLECTUAL ☐ VOCATIONAL
☐ SOCIAL   ☐ FINANCIAL   ☐ AVOCATIONAL   ☐ EMOTIONAL

_____
_____
_____
_____

My Top 3 Motivations

The Reward
How will you celebrate the achievement of your Goal!

_____
_____
_____

My first 3 Steps

_____
_____
_____

Streack Tracker   Check off your progress.

1	2	3	4	5	6	7	8	9	10	11	12	13	14	15	16	17	18	19	20	21
22	23	24	25	26	27	28	29	30	31	32	33	34	35	36	37	38	39	40	41	42
43	44	45	46	47	48	49	50	51	52	53	54	55	56	57	58	59	60	61	62	63
64	65	66	67	68	69	70	71	72	73	74	75	76	77	78	79	80	81	82	83	84
85	86	87	88	89	90	91	92	93	94	95	96	97	98	99	100	101	102	103	104	105

Write your Habit Goal

☐ Q1 ☐ Q2 ☐ Q3 ☐ Q4   Deadline _____

Domain of Life this will affect: ☐ SPIRITUAL   ☐ PARENTAL
☐ MARITAL   ☐ PHYSICAL   ☐ INTELLECTUAL   ☐ VOCATIONAL
☐ SOCIAL   ☐ FINANCIAL   ☐ AVOCATIONAL   ☐ EMOTIONAL

_____

_____

_____

_____

_____

My Top 3 Motivations

The Reward
How will you celebrate the achievement of your Goal!

My first 3 Steps

Streack Tracker   Check off your progress.

1	2	3	4	5	6	7	8	9	10	11	12	13	14	15	16	17	18	19	20	21
22	23	24	25	26	27	28	29	30	31	32	33	34	35	36	37	38	39	40	41	42
43	44	45	46	47	48	49	50	51	52	53	54	55	56	57	58	59	60	61	62	63
64	65	66	67	68	69	70	71	72	73	74	75	76	77	78	79	80	81	82	83	84
85	86	87	88	89	90	91	92	93	94	95	96	97	98	99	100	101	102	103	104	105

Write your Habit Goal

☐ Q1 ☐ Q2 ☐ Q3 ☐ Q4   Deadline _____

Domain of Life this will affect: ☐ SPIRITUAL   ☐ PARENTAL
☐ MARITAL   ☐ PHYSICAL   ☐ INTELLECTUAL   ☐ VOCATIONAL
☐ SOCIAL   ☐ FINANCIAL   ☐ AVOCATIONAL   ☐ EMOTIONAL

_____
_____
_____
_____
_____

My Top 3 Motivations

The Reward
How will you celebrate the achievement of your Goal!

My first 3 Steps

Streack Tracker   Check off your progress.

1	2	3	4	5	6	7	8	9	10	11	12	13	14	15	16	17	18	19	20	21
22	23	24	25	26	27	28	29	30	31	32	33	34	35	36	37	38	39	40	41	42
43	44	45	46	47	48	49	50	51	52	53	54	55	56	57	58	59	60	61	62	63
64	65	66	67	68	69	70	71	72	73	74	75	76	77	78	79	80	81	82	83	84
85	86	87	88	89	90	91	92	93	94	95	96	97	98	99	100	101	102	103	104	105

Write your Habit Goal

☐ Q1 ☐ Q2 ☐ Q3 ☐ Q4   Deadline _____

Domain of Life this will affect: ☐ SPIRITUAL   ☐ PARENTAL
☐ MARITAL   ☐ PHYSICAL   ☐ INTELLECTUAL   ☐ VOCATIONAL
☐ SOCIAL   ☐ FINANCIAL   ☐ AVOCATIONAL   ☐ EMOTIONAL

_____
_____
_____
_____
_____

My Top 3 Motivations

The Reward
How will you celebrate the achievement of your Goal!

_____
_____
_____

My first 3 Steps

_____
_____
_____

Streack Tracker — Check off your progress.

1	2	3	4	5	6	7	8	9	10	11	12	13	14	15	16	17	18	19	20	21
22	23	24	25	26	27	28	29	30	31	32	33	34	35	36	37	38	39	40	41	42
43	44	45	46	47	48	49	50	51	52	53	54	55	56	57	58	59	60	61	62	63
64	65	66	67	68	69	70	71	72	73	74	75	76	77	78	79	80	81	82	83	84
85	86	87	88	89	90	91	92	93	94	95	96	97	98	99	100	101	102	103	104	105

Write your Habit Goal

☐ Q1 ☐ Q2 ☐ Q3 ☐ Q4   Deadline _____

Domain of Life this will affect: ☐ SPIRITUAL   ☐ PARENTAL
☐ MARITAL   ☐ PHYSICAL   ☐ INTELLECTUAL   ☐ VOCATIONAL
☐ SOCIAL   ☐ FINANCIAL   ☐ AVOCATIONAL   ☐ EMOTIONAL

_____
_____
_____
_____

My Top 3 Motivations

The Reward
How will you celebrate the achievement of your Goal!

My first 3 Steps

Streack Tracker   Check off your progress.

1	2	3	4	5	6	7	8	9	10	11	12	13	14	15	16	17	18	19	20	21
22	23	24	25	26	27	28	29	30	31	32	33	34	35	36	37	38	39	40	41	42
43	44	45	46	47	48	49	50	51	52	53	54	55	56	57	58	59	60	61	62	63
64	65	66	67	68	69	70	71	72	73	74	75	76	77	78	79	80	81	82	83	84
85	86	87	88	89	90	91	92	93	94	95	96	97	98	99	100	101	102	103	104	105

Write your Habit Goal

☐ Q1 ☐ Q2 ☐ Q3 ☐ Q4   Deadline _____

Domain of Life this will affect: ☐ SPIRITUAL   ☐ PARENTAL
☐ MARITAL   ☐ PHYSICAL   ☐ INTELLECTUAL   ☐ VOCATIONAL
☐ SOCIAL   ☐ FINANCIAL   ☐ AVOCATIONAL   ☐ EMOTIONAL

_____
_____
_____
_____
_____

My Top 3 Motivations

The Reward
How will you celebrate the achievement of your Goal!

_____
_____
_____

My first 3 Steps

_____
_____
_____

Streack Tracker   Check off your progress.

1	2	3	4	5	6	7	8	9	10	11	12	13	14	15	16	17	18	19	20	21
22	23	24	25	26	27	28	29	30	31	32	33	34	35	36	37	38	39	40	41	42
43	44	45	46	47	48	49	50	51	52	53	54	55	56	57	58	59	60	61	62	63
64	65	66	67	68	69	70	71	72	73	74	75	76	77	78	79	80	81	82	83	84
85	86	87	88	89	90	91	92	93	94	95	96	97	98	99	100	101	102	103	104	105

Morning Ritual

- [ ]
- [ ]
- [ ]
- [ ]
- [ ]
- [ ]
- [ ]
- [ ]
- [ ]

Evening Ritual

- [ ]
- [ ]
- [ ]
- [ ]
- [ ]
- [ ]
- [ ]
- [ ]
- [ ]

Exercise Ritual

- [ ]
- [ ]
- [ ]
- [ ]
- [ ]
- [ ]
- [ ]
- [ ]
- [ ]

Study Ritual

- [ ]
- [ ]
- [ ]
- [ ]
- [ ]
- [ ]
- [ ]
- [ ]
- [ ]

MONTH _____

Top 3 priorities this month :

- [ ] _____
- [ ] _____
- [ ] _____

Things to schedule:

- [ ] Hosting

- [ ] Mentoring

- [ ] Team Meeting

- [ ] Rest

- [ ] Life-Giving

NOTES

SUNDAY	MONDAY	TUESDAY
For I know the plans I have for you, declares the LORD, plans for welfare and not for evil, to give you a future and a hope. - Jeremiah 29:11	☐	
☐	☐	☐
☐	☐	☐
☐	☐	☐
☐	☐	☐
☐	☐	☐

WEDNESDAY	THURSDAY	FRIDAY	SATURDAY

Weekly Time Map

Top 3 priorities this week:

Time		Monday	Tuesday	Wednesday
4 a.m.	:00			
	:30			
5 a.m.	:00			
	:30			
6 a.m.	:00			
	:30			
7 a.m.	:00			
	:30			
8 a.m.	:00			
	:30			
9 a.m.	:00			
	:30			
10 a.m.	:00			
	:30			
11 a.m.	:00			
	:30			
12 p.m.	:00			
	:30			
1 p.m.	:00			
	:30			
2 p.m.	:00			
	:30			
3 p.m.	:00			
	:30			
4 p.m.	:00			
	:30			
5 p.m.	:00			
	:30			
6 p.m.	:00			
	:30			
7 p.m.	:00			
	:30			
8 p.m.	:00			
	:30			
9 p.m.	:00			
	:30			
10 p.m.	:00			
	:30			

Thursday	Friday	Saturday	Sunday

Plan the Day to Achieve the Most Important Goals.

Monday

Top 3 Priorities Today:
- [ ]
- [ ]
- [ ]

Hour of Power
- [ ] Prayer / 20 min
- [ ] Read / 20 min
- [ ] Exercise / 20 min

Homework:
- [ ]
- [ ]
- [ ]
- [ ]
- [ ]
- [ ]

To Do:
- [ ]
- [ ]
- [ ]
- [ ]
- [ ]
- [ ]
- [ ]
- [ ]
- [ ]
- [ ]
- [ ]
- [ ]
- [ ]
- [ ]
- [ ]
- [ ]
- [ ]
- [ ]
- [ ]
- [ ]

Appointments/Dates
- [ ]
- [ ]
- [ ]

Calls/Emails
- [ ]
- [ ]
- [ ]
- [ ]
- [ ]
- [ ]
- [ ]

Today I'm Grateful for:

Ideas/Plans

➡ = Forward   X = Delete   ✓ = Completed

Daily Breakdown:

4 AM	
5 AM	
6 AM	
7 AM	
8 AM	
9 AM	
10 AM	
11 AM	
12 PM	
1 PM	
2 PM	
3 PM	
4 PM	
5 PM	
6 PM	
7 PM	
8 PM	
9 PM	
10 PM	

NOTES

Plan the Day to Achieve the Most Important Goals.	Tuesday

Top 3 Priorities Today:
- [ ]
- [ ]
- [ ]

Hour of Power
- [ ] Prayer / 20 min
- [ ] Read / 20 min
- [ ] Exercise / 20 min

Homework:
- [ ]
- [ ]
- [ ]
- [ ]
- [ ]
- [ ]

To Do:
- [ ]
- [ ]
- [ ]
- [ ]
- [ ]
- [ ]
- [ ]
- [ ]
- [ ]
- [ ]
- [ ]
- [ ]
- [ ]
- [ ]
- [ ]
- [ ]
- [ ]
- [ ]
- [ ]
- [ ]

Appointments/Dates
- [ ]
- [ ]
- [ ]

Calls/Emails
- [ ]
- [ ]
- [ ]
- [ ]
- [ ]
- [ ]
- [ ]

Today I'm Grateful for:

Ideas/Plans

➡ = Forward   X = Delete   ✓ = Completed

Daily Breakdown:

4 AM	
5 AM	
6 AM	
7 AM	
8 AM	
9 AM	
10 AM	
11 AM	
12 PM	
1 PM	
2 PM	
3 PM	
4 PM	
5 PM	
6 PM	
7 PM	
8 PM	
9 PM	
10 PM	

NOTES

Plan the Day to Achieve the Most Important Goals.	Wednesday

Top 3 Priorities Today:	Hour of Power	Homework:
☐	☐ Prayer / 20 min	☐
☐	☐ Read / 20 min	☐
☐	☐ Exercise / 20 min	☐

To Do:

☐
☐
☐
☐
☐
☐
☐
☐
☐
☐
☐
☐
☐
☐
☐
☐
☐
☐
☐
☐
☐

Appointments/Dates
☐
☐
☐

Calls/Emails
☐
☐
☐
☐
☐
☐
☐

Today I'm Grateful for:

Ideas/Plans

➡ = Forward   X = Delete   ✓ = Completed

Daily Breakdown:

4 AM
5 AM
6 AM
7 AM
8 AM
9 AM
10 AM
11 AM
12 PM
1 PM
2 PM
3 PM
4 PM
5 PM
6 PM
7 PM
8 PM
9 PM
10 PM

NOTES

Plan the Day to Achieve the Most Important Goals.

Thursday

Top 3 Priorities Today:
- [ ]
- [ ]
- [ ]

Hour of Power
- [ ] Prayer / 20 min
- [ ] Read / 20 min
- [ ] Exercise / 20 min

Homework:
- [ ]
- [ ]
- [ ]
- [ ]
- [ ]
- [ ]

To Do:
- [ ]
- [ ]
- [ ]
- [ ]
- [ ]
- [ ]
- [ ]
- [ ]
- [ ]
- [ ]
- [ ]
- [ ]
- [ ]
- [ ]
- [ ]
- [ ]
- [ ]
- [ ]
- [ ]
- [ ]

Appointments/Dates
- [ ]
- [ ]
- [ ]

Calls/Emails
- [ ]
- [ ]
- [ ]
- [ ]
- [ ]
- [ ]
- [ ]

Today I'm Grateful for:

Ideas/Plans

➡ = Forward   X = Delete   ✓ = Completed

Daily Breakdown:

NOTES

4 AM
5 AM
6 AM
7 AM
8 AM
9 AM
10 AM
11 AM
12 PM
1 PM
2 PM
3 PM
4 PM
5 PM
6 PM
7 PM
8 PM
9 PM
10 PM

Plan the Day to Achieve the Most Important Goals.	Friday

Top 3 Priorities Today:	Hour of Power	Homework:
☐	☐ Prayer / 20 min	☐
☐	☐ Read / 20 min	☐
☐	☐ Exercise / 20 min	☐

To Do:

☐
☐
☐
☐
☐
☐
☐
☐
☐
☐
☐
☐
☐
☐
☐
☐
☐
☐
☐
☐
☐

Appointments/Dates

☐
☐
☐

Calls/Emails

☐
☐
☐
☐
☐
☐
☐

Today I'm Grateful for:

Ideas/Plans

➡ = Forward   X = Delete   ✓ = Completed

Daily Breakdown:

4 AM	
5 AM	
6 AM	
7 AM	
8 AM	
9 AM	
10 AM	
11 AM	
12 PM	
1 PM	
2 PM	
3 PM	
4 PM	
5 PM	
6 PM	
7 PM	
8 PM	
9 PM	
10 PM	

NOTES

Weekly Reflections

How do you plan to rest this weekend?

What will you NOT do in order to find rest?

What will you do that is Life-Giving?

List 3 -5 Relationships you want to invest in this weekend:
- [ ]
- [ ]
- [ ]
- [ ]
- [ ]

How will you invest in those relationships?
- [ ]
- [ ]
- [ ]
- [ ]
- [ ]

What have I read/heard this week that stood out?

How will I implement what I learned this week?

What are my 3 Biggest Wins for this week?
- [ ]
- [ ]
- [ ]

What are my top 3 priorities for next week?
- [ ]
- [ ]
- [ ]

| What God has told me to do this year: | What God did for me this week: |

What God is saying Now!

| What am I asking God for this week? | My next Steps to obey what God has said: |

Plan the Day to Achieve the Most Important Goals.

Saturday

Top 3 Priorities Today:
- [ ]
- [ ]
- [ ]

Hour of Power
- [ ] Prayer / 20 min
- [ ] Read / 20 min
- [ ] Exercise / 20 min

Homework:
- [ ]
- [ ]
- [ ]
- [ ]
- [ ]
- [ ]

To Do:
- [ ]
- [ ]
- [ ]
- [ ]
- [ ]
- [ ]
- [ ]
- [ ]
- [ ]
- [ ]
- [ ]
- [ ]
- [ ]
- [ ]
- [ ]
- [ ]
- [ ]
- [ ]
- [ ]
- [ ]
- [ ]
- [ ]

Appointments/Dates
- [ ]
- [ ]
- [ ]

Calls/Emails
- [ ]
- [ ]
- [ ]
- [ ]
- [ ]
- [ ]
- [ ]

Today I'm Grateful for:

Ideas/Plans

➡ = Forward   X = Delete   ✓ = Completed

Daily Breakdown:

4 AM	
5 AM	
6 AM	
7 AM	
8 AM	
9 AM	
10 AM	
11 AM	
12 PM	
1 PM	
2 PM	
3 PM	
4 PM	
5 PM	
6 PM	
7 PM	
8 PM	
9 PM	
10 PM	

NOTES

Plan the Day to Achieve the Most Important Goals.

Sunday

Top 3 Priorities Today:
- [ ]
- [ ]
- [ ]

Hour of Power
- [ ] Prayer / 20 min
- [ ] Read / 20 min
- [ ] Exercise / 20 min

Homework:
- [ ]
- [ ]
- [ ]
- [ ]
- [ ]
- [ ]

To Do:
- [ ]
- [ ]
- [ ]
- [ ]
- [ ]
- [ ]
- [ ]
- [ ]
- [ ]
- [ ]
- [ ]
- [ ]
- [ ]
- [ ]
- [ ]
- [ ]
- [ ]
- [ ]
- [ ]
- [ ]
- [ ]
- [ ]

Appointments/Dates
- [ ]
- [ ]
- [ ]

Calls/Emails
- [ ]
- [ ]
- [ ]
- [ ]
- [ ]
- [ ]
- [ ]

Today I'm Grateful for:

Ideas/Plans

➡ = Forward   X = Delete   ✓ = Completed

Daily Breakdown:

4 AM
5 AM
6 AM
7 AM
8 AM
9 AM
10 AM
11 AM
12 PM
1 PM
2 PM
3 PM
4 PM
5 PM
6 PM
7 PM
8 PM
9 PM
10 PM

NOTES

Weekly Time Map

Top 3 priorities this week:

Time		Monday	Tuesday	Wednesday
4 a.m.	:00			
	:30			
5 a.m.	:00			
	:30			
6 a.m.	:00			
	:30			
7 a.m.	:00			
	:30			
8 a.m.	:00			
	:30			
9 a.m.	:00			
	:30			
10 a.m.	:00			
	:30			
11 a.m.	:00			
	:30			
12 p.m.	:00			
	:30			
1 p.m.	:00			
	:30			
2 p.m.	:00			
	:30			
3 p.m.	:00			
	:30			
4 p.m.	:00			
	:30			
5 p.m.	:00			
	:30			
6 p.m.	:00			
	:30			
7 p.m.	:00			
	:30			
8 p.m.	:00			
	:30			
9 p.m.	:00			
	:30			
10 p.m.	:00			
	:30			

☐ Thursday	☐ Friday	☐ Saturday	Sunday

Plan the Day to Achieve the Most Important Goals.

Monday

Top 3 Priorities Today:
- [ ]
- [ ]
- [ ]

Hour of Power
- [ ] Prayer / 20 min
- [ ] Read / 20 min
- [ ] Exercise / 20 min

Homework:
- [ ]
- [ ]
- [ ]
- [ ]
- [ ]
- [ ]

To Do:
- [ ]
- [ ]
- [ ]
- [ ]
- [ ]
- [ ]
- [ ]
- [ ]
- [ ]
- [ ]
- [ ]
- [ ]
- [ ]
- [ ]
- [ ]
- [ ]
- [ ]
- [ ]
- [ ]
- [ ]

Appointments/Dates
- [ ]
- [ ]
- [ ]

Calls/Emails
- [ ]
- [ ]
- [ ]
- [ ]
- [ ]
- [ ]
- [ ]

Today I'm Grateful for:

Ideas/Plans

➡ = Forward   X = Delete   ✓ = Completed

Daily Breakdown:

4 AM	
5 AM	
6 AM	
7 AM	
8 AM	
9 AM	
10 AM	
11 AM	
12 PM	
1 PM	
2 PM	
3 PM	
4 PM	
5 PM	
6 PM	
7 PM	
8 PM	
9 PM	
10 PM	

NOTES

Plan the Day to Achieve the Most Important Goals.

Tuesday

Top 3 Priorities Today:
- ☐
- ☐
- ☐

Hour of Power
- ☐ Prayer / 20 min
- ☐ Read / 20 min
- ☐ Exercise / 20 min

Homework:
- ☐
- ☐
- ☐
- ☐
- ☐
- ☐

To Do:
- ☐
- ☐
- ☐
- ☐
- ☐
- ☐
- ☐
- ☐
- ☐
- ☐
- ☐
- ☐
- ☐
- ☐
- ☐
- ☐
- ☐
- ☐
- ☐
- ☐
- ☐

Appointments/Dates
- ☐
- ☐
- ☐

Calls/Emails
- ☐
- ☐
- ☐
- ☐
- ☐
- ☐
- ☐

Today I'm Grateful for:

Ideas/Plans

➡ = Forward   X = Delete   ✓ = Completed

Daily Breakdown:

4 AM	
5 AM	
6 AM	
7 AM	
8 AM	
9 AM	
10 AM	
11 AM	
12 PM	
1 PM	
2 PM	
3 PM	
4 PM	
5 PM	
6 PM	
7 PM	
8 PM	
9 PM	
10 PM	

NOTES

Plan the Day to Achieve the Most Important Goals.

Wednesday

Top 3 Priorities Today:
- [ ]
- [ ]
- [ ]

Hour of Power
- [ ] Prayer / 20 min
- [ ] Read / 20 min
- [ ] Exercise / 20 min

Homework:
- [ ]
- [ ]
- [ ]
- [ ]
- [ ]
- [ ]

To Do:
- [ ]
- [ ]
- [ ]
- [ ]
- [ ]
- [ ]
- [ ]
- [ ]
- [ ]
- [ ]
- [ ]
- [ ]
- [ ]
- [ ]
- [ ]
- [ ]
- [ ]
- [ ]
- [ ]
- [ ]
- [ ]

Appointments/Dates
- [ ]
- [ ]
- [ ]

Calls/Emails
- [ ]
- [ ]
- [ ]
- [ ]
- [ ]
- [ ]
- [ ]

Today I'm Grateful for:

Ideas/Plans

➡ = Forward   X = Delete   ✓ = Completed

Daily Breakdown:

4 AM
5 AM
6 AM
7 AM
8 AM
9 AM
10 AM
11 AM
12 PM
1 PM
2 PM
3 PM
4 PM
5 PM
6 PM
7 PM
8 PM
9 PM
10 PM

NOTES

Plan the Day to Achieve the Most Important Goals.

Thursday

Top 3 Priorities Today:
- [ ]
- [ ]
- [ ]

Hour of Power
- [ ] Prayer / 20 min
- [ ] Read / 20 min
- [ ] Exercise / 20 min

Homework:
- [ ]
- [ ]
- [ ]
- [ ]
- [ ]
- [ ]

To Do:
- [ ]
- [ ]
- [ ]
- [ ]
- [ ]
- [ ]
- [ ]
- [ ]
- [ ]
- [ ]
- [ ]
- [ ]
- [ ]
- [ ]
- [ ]
- [ ]
- [ ]
- [ ]
- [ ]
- [ ]

Appointments/Dates
- [ ]
- [ ]
- [ ]

Calls/Emails
- [ ]
- [ ]
- [ ]
- [ ]
- [ ]
- [ ]
- [ ]

Today I'm Grateful for:

Ideas/Plans

➡ = Forward   X = Delete   ✓ = Completed

Daily Breakdown:

4 AM	
5 AM	
6 AM	
7 AM	
8 AM	
9 AM	
10 AM	
11 AM	
12 PM	
1 PM	
2 PM	
3 PM	
4 PM	
5 PM	
6 PM	
7 PM	
8 PM	
9 PM	
10 PM	

NOTES

Plan the Day to Achieve the Most Important Goals.

Friday

Top 3 Priorities Today:
- [ ]
- [ ]
- [ ]

Hour of Power
- [ ] Prayer / 20 min
- [ ] Read / 20 min
- [ ] Exercise / 20 min

Homework:
- [ ]
- [ ]
- [ ]
- [ ]
- [ ]
- [ ]

To Do:
- [ ]
- [ ]
- [ ]
- [ ]
- [ ]
- [ ]
- [ ]
- [ ]
- [ ]
- [ ]
- [ ]
- [ ]
- [ ]
- [ ]
- [ ]
- [ ]
- [ ]
- [ ]
- [ ]
- [ ]

Appointments/Dates
- [ ]
- [ ]
- [ ]

Calls/Emails
- [ ]
- [ ]
- [ ]
- [ ]
- [ ]
- [ ]
- [ ]

Today I'm Grateful for:

Ideas/Plans

➡ = Forward   X = Delete   ✓ = Completed

Daily Breakdown:

NOTES

4 AM
5 AM
6 AM
7 AM
8 AM
9 AM
10 AM
11 AM
12 PM
1 PM
2 PM
3 PM
4 PM
5 PM
6 PM
7 PM
8 PM
9 PM
10 PM

Weekly Reflections

How do you plan to rest this weekend?

What will you NOT do in order to find rest?

What will you do that is Life-Giving?

List 3 -5 Relationships you want to invest in this weekend:
- [ ]
- [ ]
- [ ]
- [ ]
- [ ]

How will you invest in those relationships?
- [ ]
- [ ]
- [ ]
- [ ]
- [ ]

What have I read/heard this week that stood out?

How will I implement what I learned this week?

What are my 3 Biggest Wins for this week?
- [ ]
- [ ]
- [ ]

What are my top 3 priorities for next week?
- [ ]
- [ ]
- [ ]

| What God has told me to do this year: | What God did for me this week: |

What God is saying Now!

| What am I asking God for this week? | My next Steps to obey what God has said: |

Plan the Day to Achieve the Most Important Goals.

Saturday

Top 3 Priorities Today:
- [ ]
- [ ]
- [ ]

Hour of Power
- [ ] Prayer / 20 min
- [ ] Read / 20 min
- [ ] Exercise / 20 min

Homework:
- [ ]
- [ ]
- [ ]
- [ ]
- [ ]
- [ ]

To Do:
- [ ]
- [ ]
- [ ]
- [ ]
- [ ]
- [ ]
- [ ]
- [ ]
- [ ]
- [ ]
- [ ]
- [ ]
- [ ]
- [ ]
- [ ]
- [ ]
- [ ]
- [ ]
- [ ]
- [ ]

Appointments/Dates
- [ ]
- [ ]
- [ ]

Calls/Emails
- [ ]
- [ ]
- [ ]
- [ ]
- [ ]
- [ ]
- [ ]

Today I'm Grateful for:

Ideas/Plans

➡ = Forward   X = Delete   ✓ = Completed

Daily Breakdown:

4 AM
5 AM
6 AM
7 AM
8 AM
9 AM
10 AM
11 AM
12 PM
1 PM
2 PM
3 PM
4 PM
5 PM
6 PM
7 PM
8 PM
9 PM
10 PM

NOTES

Plan the Day to Achieve the Most Important Goals.

Sunday

Top 3 Priorities Today:
- [ ]
- [ ]
- [ ]

Hour of Power
- [ ] Prayer / 20 min
- [ ] Read / 20 min
- [ ] Exercise / 20 min

Homework:
- [ ]
- [ ]
- [ ]
- [ ]
- [ ]
- [ ]

To Do:
- [ ]
- [ ]
- [ ]
- [ ]
- [ ]
- [ ]
- [ ]
- [ ]
- [ ]
- [ ]
- [ ]
- [ ]
- [ ]
- [ ]
- [ ]
- [ ]
- [ ]
- [ ]
- [ ]
- [ ]

Appointments/Dates
- [ ]
- [ ]
- [ ]

Calls/Emails
- [ ]
- [ ]
- [ ]
- [ ]
- [ ]
- [ ]
- [ ]

Today I'm Grateful for:

Ideas/Plans

➡ = Forward   X = Delete   ✓ = Completed

Daily Breakdown:

4 AM	
5 AM	
6 AM	
7 AM	
8 AM	
9 AM	
10 AM	
11 AM	
12 PM	
1 PM	
2 PM	
3 PM	
4 PM	
5 PM	
6 PM	
7 PM	
8 PM	
9 PM	
10 PM	

NOTES

Weekly Time Map

Top 3 priorities this week:

Time		Monday	Tuesday	Wednesday
4 a.m.	:00 :30			
5 a.m.	:00 :30			
6 a.m.	:00 :30			
7 a.m.	:00 :30			
8 a.m.	:00 :30			
9 a.m.	:00 :30			
10 a.m.	:00 :30			
11 a.m.	:00 :30			
12 p.m.	:00 :30			
1 p.m.	:00 :30			
2 p.m.	:00 :30			
3 p.m.	:00 :30			
4 p.m.	:00 :30			
5 p.m.	:00 :30			
6 p.m.	:00 :30			
7 p.m.	:00 :30			
8 p.m.	:00 :30			
9 p.m.	:00 :30			
10 p.m.	:00 :30			

☐ Thursday	☐ Friday	☐ Saturday	☐ Sunday

Plan the Day to Achieve the Most Important Goals.

Monday

Top 3 Priorities Today:
- [ ]
- [ ]
- [ ]

Hour of Power
- [ ] Prayer / 20 min
- [ ] Read / 20 min
- [ ] Exercise / 20 min

Homework:
- [ ]
- [ ]
- [ ]
- [ ]
- [ ]
- [ ]

To Do:
- [ ]
- [ ]
- [ ]
- [ ]
- [ ]
- [ ]
- [ ]
- [ ]
- [ ]
- [ ]
- [ ]
- [ ]
- [ ]
- [ ]
- [ ]
- [ ]
- [ ]
- [ ]
- [ ]
- [ ]
- [ ]

Appointments/Dates
- [ ]
- [ ]
- [ ]

Calls/Emails
- [ ]
- [ ]
- [ ]
- [ ]
- [ ]
- [ ]
- [ ]

Today I'm Grateful for:

Ideas/Plans

➡ = Forward   X = Delete   ✓ = Completed

Daily Breakdown:

NOTES

4 AM
5 AM
6 AM
7 AM
8 AM
9 AM
10 AM
11 AM
12 PM
1 PM
2 PM
3 PM
4 PM
5 PM
6 PM
7 PM
8 PM
9 PM
10 PM

Plan the Day to Achieve the Most Important Goals.

Tuesday

Top 3 Priorities Today:
- [ ]
- [ ]
- [ ]

Hour of Power
- [ ] Prayer / 20 min
- [ ] Read / 20 min
- [ ] Exercise / 20 min

Homework:
- [ ]
- [ ]
- [ ]
- [ ]
- [ ]
- [ ]

To Do:
- [ ]
- [ ]
- [ ]
- [ ]
- [ ]
- [ ]
- [ ]
- [ ]
- [ ]
- [ ]
- [ ]
- [ ]
- [ ]
- [ ]
- [ ]
- [ ]
- [ ]
- [ ]
- [ ]
- [ ]

Appointments/Dates
- [ ]
- [ ]
- [ ]

Calls/Emails
- [ ]
- [ ]
- [ ]
- [ ]
- [ ]
- [ ]
- [ ]

Today I'm Grateful for:

Ideas/Plans

➡ = Forward   X = Delete   ✓ = Completed

Daily Breakdown:

4 AM	
5 AM	
6 AM	
7 AM	
8 AM	
9 AM	
10 AM	
11 AM	
12 PM	
1 PM	
2 PM	
3 PM	
4 PM	
5 PM	
6 PM	
7 PM	
8 PM	
9 PM	
10 PM	

NOTES

Plan the Day to Achieve the Most Important Goals.

Wednesday

Top 3 Priorities Today:
- [ ]
- [ ]
- [ ]

Hour of Power
- [ ] Prayer / 20 min
- [ ] Read / 20 min
- [ ] Exercise / 20 min

Homework:
- [ ]
- [ ]
- [ ]
- [ ]
- [ ]
- [ ]

To Do:
- [ ]
- [ ]
- [ ]
- [ ]
- [ ]
- [ ]
- [ ]
- [ ]
- [ ]
- [ ]
- [ ]
- [ ]
- [ ]
- [ ]
- [ ]
- [ ]
- [ ]
- [ ]
- [ ]
- [ ]

Appointments/Dates
- [ ]
- [ ]
- [ ]

Calls/Emails
- [ ]
- [ ]
- [ ]
- [ ]
- [ ]
- [ ]
- [ ]

Today I'm Grateful for:

Ideas/Plans

➡ = Forward   X = Delete   ✓ = Completed

Daily Breakdown:

NOTES

4 AM
5 AM
6 AM
7 AM
8 AM
9 AM
10 AM
11 AM
12 PM
1 PM
2 PM
3 PM
4 PM
5 PM
6 PM
7 PM
8 PM
9 PM
10 PM

Plan the Day to Achieve the Most Important Goals.

Thursday

Top 3 Priorities Today:
- ☐
- ☐
- ☐

Hour of Power
- ☐ Prayer / 20 min
- ☐ Read / 20 min
- ☐ Exercise / 20 min

Homework:
- ☐
- ☐
- ☐
- ☐
- ☐
- ☐

To Do:
- ☐
- ☐
- ☐
- ☐
- ☐
- ☐
- ☐
- ☐
- ☐
- ☐
- ☐
- ☐
- ☐
- ☐
- ☐
- ☐
- ☐
- ☐
- ☐
- ☐

Appointments/Dates
- ☐
- ☐
- ☐

Calls/Emails
- ☐
- ☐
- ☐
- ☐
- ☐
- ☐
- ☐

Today I'm Grateful for:

Ideas/Plans

➡ = Forward   X = Delete   ✓ = Completed

Daily Breakdown:

4 AM	
5 AM	
6 AM	
7 AM	
8 AM	
9 AM	
10 AM	
11 AM	
12 PM	
1 PM	
2 PM	
3 PM	
4 PM	
5 PM	
6 PM	
7 PM	
8 PM	
9 PM	
10 PM	

NOTES

Plan the Day to Achieve the Most Important Goals.

Friday

Top 3 Priorities Today:
- [ ]
- [ ]
- [ ]

Hour of Power
- [ ] Prayer / 20 min
- [ ] Read / 20 min
- [ ] Exercise / 20 min

Homework:
- [ ]
- [ ]
- [ ]
- [ ]
- [ ]
- [ ]

To Do:
- [ ]
- [ ]
- [ ]
- [ ]
- [ ]
- [ ]
- [ ]
- [ ]
- [ ]
- [ ]
- [ ]
- [ ]
- [ ]
- [ ]
- [ ]
- [ ]
- [ ]
- [ ]
- [ ]
- [ ]
- [ ]

Appointments/Dates
- [ ]
- [ ]
- [ ]

Calls/Emails
- [ ]
- [ ]
- [ ]
- [ ]
- [ ]
- [ ]
- [ ]

Today I'm Grateful for:

Ideas/Plans

➡ = Forward   X = Delete   ✓ = Completed

Daily Breakdown:

4 AM	
5 AM	
6 AM	
7 AM	
8 AM	
9 AM	
10 AM	
11 AM	
12 PM	
1 PM	
2 PM	
3 PM	
4 PM	
5 PM	
6 PM	
7 PM	
8 PM	
9 PM	
10 PM	

NOTES

Weekly Reflections

How do you plan to rest this weekend?

What will you NOT do in order to find rest?

What will you do that is Life-Giving?

List 3 -5 Relationships you want to invest in this weekend:
- [ ]
- [ ]
- [ ]
- [ ]
- [ ]

How will you invest in those relationships?
- [ ]
- [ ]
- [ ]
- [ ]
- [ ]

What have I read/heard this week that stood out?

How will I implement what I learned this week?

What are my 3 Biggest Wins for this week?
- [ ]
- [ ]
- [ ]

What are my top 3 priorities for next week?
- [ ]
- [ ]
- [ ]

| What God has told me to do this year: | What God did for me this week: |

What God is saying Now!

| What am I asking God for this week? | My next Steps to obey what God has said: |

Plan the Day to Achieve the Most Important Goals.

Saturday

Top 3 Priorities Today:
- ☐
- ☐
- ☐

Hour of Power
- ☐ Prayer / 20 min
- ☐ Read / 20 min
- ☐ Exercise / 20 min

Homework:
- ☐
- ☐
- ☐
- ☐
- ☐
- ☐

To Do:
- ☐
- ☐
- ☐
- ☐
- ☐
- ☐
- ☐
- ☐
- ☐
- ☐
- ☐
- ☐
- ☐
- ☐
- ☐
- ☐
- ☐
- ☐
- ☐
- ☐
- ☐

Appointments/Dates
- ☐
- ☐
- ☐

Calls/Emails
- ☐
- ☐
- ☐
- ☐
- ☐
- ☐
- ☐

Today I'm Grateful for:

Ideas/Plans

➡ = Forward   X = Delete   ✓ = Completed

Daily Breakdown:

4 AM	
5 AM	
6 AM	
7 AM	
8 AM	
9 AM	
10 AM	
11 AM	
12 PM	
1 PM	
2 PM	
3 PM	
4 PM	
5 PM	
6 PM	
7 PM	
8 PM	
9 PM	
10 PM	

NOTES

Plan the Day to Achieve the Most Important Goals.

Sunday

Top 3 Priorities Today:
- [ ]
- [ ]
- [ ]

Hour of Power
- [ ] Prayer / 20 min
- [ ] Read / 20 min
- [ ] Exercise / 20 min

Homework:
- [ ]
- [ ]
- [ ]
- [ ]
- [ ]
- [ ]

To Do:
- [ ]
- [ ]
- [ ]
- [ ]
- [ ]
- [ ]
- [ ]
- [ ]
- [ ]
- [ ]
- [ ]
- [ ]
- [ ]
- [ ]
- [ ]
- [ ]
- [ ]
- [ ]
- [ ]
- [ ]

Appointments/Dates
- [ ]
- [ ]
- [ ]

Calls/Emails
- [ ]
- [ ]
- [ ]
- [ ]
- [ ]
- [ ]
- [ ]

Today I'm Grateful for:

Ideas/Plans

➡ = Forward   X = Delete   ✓ = Completed

Daily Breakdown:

4 AM
5 AM
6 AM
7 AM
8 AM
9 AM
10 AM
11 AM
12 PM
1 PM
2 PM
3 PM
4 PM
5 PM
6 PM
7 PM
8 PM
9 PM
10 PM

NOTES

Weekly Time Map

Top 3 priorities this week:

Time		Monday	Tuesday	Wednesday
4 a.m.	:00			
	:30			
5 a.m.	:00			
	:30			
6 a.m.	:00			
	:30			
7 a.m.	:00			
	:30			
8 a.m.	:00			
	:30			
9 a.m.	:00			
	:30			
10 a.m.	:00			
	:30			
11 a.m.	:00			
	:30			
12 p.m.	:00			
	:30			
1 p.m.	:00			
	:30			
2 p.m.	:00			
	:30			
3 p.m.	:00			
	:30			
4 p.m.	:00			
	:30			
5 p.m.	:00			
	:30			
6 p.m.	:00			
	:30			
7 p.m.	:00			
	:30			
8 p.m.	:00			
	:30			
9 p.m.	:00			
	:30			
10 p.m.	:00			
	:30			

☐ Thursday	☐ Friday	☐ Saturday	☐ Sunday

Plan the Day to Achieve the Most Important Goals.

Monday

Top 3 Priorities Today:
- [ ]
- [ ]
- [ ]

Hour of Power
- [ ] Prayer / 20 min
- [ ] Read / 20 min
- [ ] Exercise / 20 min

Homework:
- [ ]
- [ ]
- [ ]
- [ ]
- [ ]
- [ ]

To Do:
- [ ]
- [ ]
- [ ]
- [ ]
- [ ]
- [ ]
- [ ]
- [ ]
- [ ]
- [ ]
- [ ]
- [ ]
- [ ]
- [ ]
- [ ]
- [ ]
- [ ]
- [ ]
- [ ]
- [ ]

Appointments/Dates
- [ ]
- [ ]
- [ ]

Calls/Emails
- [ ]
- [ ]
- [ ]
- [ ]
- [ ]
- [ ]
- [ ]

Today I'm Grateful for:

Ideas/Plans

➡ = Forward   X = Delete   ✓ = Completed

Daily Breakdown:

NOTES

4 AM
5 AM
6 AM
7 AM
8 AM
9 AM
10 AM
11 AM
12 PM
1 PM
2 PM
3 PM
4 PM
5 PM
6 PM
7 PM
8 PM
9 PM
10 PM

Plan the Day to Achieve the Most Important Goals.

Tuesday

Top 3 Priorities Today:
- [ ]
- [ ]
- [ ]

Hour of Power
- [ ] Prayer / 20 min
- [ ] Read / 20 min
- [ ] Exercise / 20 min

Homework:
- [ ]
- [ ]
- [ ]
- [ ]
- [ ]
- [ ]

To Do:
- [ ]
- [ ]
- [ ]
- [ ]
- [ ]
- [ ]
- [ ]
- [ ]
- [ ]
- [ ]
- [ ]
- [ ]
- [ ]
- [ ]
- [ ]
- [ ]
- [ ]
- [ ]
- [ ]
- [ ]
- [ ]

Appointments/Dates
- [ ]
- [ ]
- [ ]

Calls/Emails
- [ ]
- [ ]
- [ ]
- [ ]
- [ ]
- [ ]
- [ ]

Today I'm Grateful for:

Ideas/Plans

➡ = Forward   X = Delete   ✓ = Completed

Daily Breakdown:

	NOTES

4 AM
5 AM
6 AM
7 AM
8 AM
9 AM
10 AM
11 AM
12 PM
1 PM
2 PM
3 PM
4 PM
5 PM
6 PM
7 PM
8 PM
9 PM
10 PM

Plan the Day to Achieve the Most Important Goals.

Wednesday

Top 3 Priorities Today:
- [ ]
- [ ]
- [ ]

Hour of Power
- [ ] Prayer / 20 min
- [ ] Read / 20 min
- [ ] Exercise / 20 min

Homework:
- [ ]
- [ ]
- [ ]
- [ ]
- [ ]
- [ ]

To Do:
- [ ]
- [ ]
- [ ]
- [ ]
- [ ]
- [ ]
- [ ]
- [ ]
- [ ]
- [ ]
- [ ]
- [ ]
- [ ]
- [ ]
- [ ]
- [ ]
- [ ]
- [ ]
- [ ]
- [ ]
- [ ]

Appointments/Dates
- [ ]
- [ ]
- [ ]

Calls/Emails
- [ ]
- [ ]
- [ ]
- [ ]
- [ ]
- [ ]
- [ ]

Today I'm Grateful for:

Ideas/Plans

➡ = Forward   X = Delete   ✓ = Completed

Daily Breakdown:

NOTES

4 AM
5 AM
6 AM
7 AM
8 AM
9 AM
10 AM
11 AM
12 PM
1 PM
2 PM
3 PM
4 PM
5 PM
6 PM
7 PM
8 PM
9 PM
10 PM

Plan the Day to Achieve the Most Important Goals.

Thursday

Top 3 Priorities Today:
- ☐
- ☐
- ☐

Hour of Power
- ☐ Prayer / 20 min
- ☐ Read / 20 min
- ☐ Exercise / 20 min

Homework:
- ☐
- ☐
- ☐
- ☐
- ☐
- ☐

To Do:
- ☐
- ☐
- ☐
- ☐
- ☐
- ☐
- ☐
- ☐
- ☐
- ☐
- ☐
- ☐
- ☐
- ☐
- ☐
- ☐
- ☐
- ☐
- ☐
- ☐
- ☐
- ☐

Appointments/Dates
- ☐
- ☐
- ☐

Calls/Emails
- ☐
- ☐
- ☐
- ☐
- ☐
- ☐
- ☐

Today I'm Grateful for:

Ideas/Plans

➡ = Forward   X = Delete   ✓ = Completed

Daily Breakdown:

NOTES

4 AM
5 AM
6 AM
7 AM
8 AM
9 AM
10 AM
11 AM
12 PM
1 PM
2 PM
3 PM
4 PM
5 PM
6 PM
7 PM
8 PM
9 PM
10 PM

Plan the Day to Achieve the Most Important Goals.

Friday

Top 3 Priorities Today:
- [ ]
- [ ]
- [ ]

Hour of Power
- [ ] Prayer / 20 min
- [ ] Read / 20 min
- [ ] Exercise / 20 min

Homework:
- [ ]
- [ ]
- [ ]
- [ ]
- [ ]
- [ ]

To Do:
- [ ]
- [ ]
- [ ]
- [ ]
- [ ]
- [ ]
- [ ]
- [ ]
- [ ]
- [ ]
- [ ]
- [ ]
- [ ]
- [ ]
- [ ]
- [ ]
- [ ]
- [ ]
- [ ]
- [ ]
- [ ]

Appointments/Dates
- [ ]
- [ ]
- [ ]

Calls/Emails
- [ ]
- [ ]
- [ ]
- [ ]
- [ ]
- [ ]
- [ ]

Today I'm Grateful for:

Ideas/Plans

➡ = Forward   X = Delete   ✓ = Completed

Daily Breakdown:

	NOTES

4 AM
5 AM
6 AM
7 AM
8 AM
9 AM
10 AM
11 AM
12 PM
1 PM
2 PM
3 PM
4 PM
5 PM
6 PM
7 PM
8 PM
9 PM
10 PM

Weekly Reflections

How do you plan to rest this weekend?

What will you NOT do in order to find rest?

What will you do that is Life-Giving?

List 3 -5 Relationships you want to invest in this weekend:
- ☐
- ☐
- ☐
- ☐
- ☐

How will you invest in those relationships?
- ☐
- ☐
- ☐
- ☐
- ☐

What have I read/heard this week that stood out?

How will I implement what I learned this week?

What are my 3 Biggest Wins for this week?
- ☐
- ☐
- ☐

What are my top 3 priorities for next week?
- ☐
- ☐
- ☐

What God has told me to do this year:	What God did for me this week:

What God is saying Now!

What am I asking God for this week?	My next Steps to obey what God has said:

Plan the Day to Achieve the Most Important Goals.

Saturday

Top 3 Priorities Today:
- [ ]
- [ ]
- [ ]

Hour of Power
- [ ] Prayer / 20 min
- [ ] Read / 20 min
- [ ] Exercise / 20 min

Homework:
- [ ]
- [ ]
- [ ]
- [ ]
- [ ]
- [ ]

To Do:
- [ ]
- [ ]
- [ ]
- [ ]
- [ ]
- [ ]
- [ ]
- [ ]
- [ ]
- [ ]
- [ ]
- [ ]
- [ ]
- [ ]
- [ ]
- [ ]
- [ ]
- [ ]
- [ ]
- [ ]

Appointments/Dates
- [ ]
- [ ]
- [ ]

Calls/Emails
- [ ]
- [ ]
- [ ]
- [ ]
- [ ]
- [ ]
- [ ]

Today I'm Grateful for:

Ideas/Plans

➡ = Forward   X = Delete   ✓ = Completed

Daily Breakdown:

4 AM
5 AM
6 AM
7 AM
8 AM
9 AM
10 AM
11 AM
12 PM
1 PM
2 PM
3 PM
4 PM
5 PM
6 PM
7 PM
8 PM
9 PM
10 PM

NOTES

Plan the Day to Achieve the Most Important Goals.

Sunday

Top 3 Priorities Today:
- [ ]
- [ ]
- [ ]

Hour of Power
- [ ] Prayer / 20 min
- [ ] Read / 20 min
- [ ] Exercise / 20 min

Homework:
- [ ]
- [ ]
- [ ]
- [ ]
- [ ]
- [ ]

To Do:
- [ ]
- [ ]
- [ ]
- [ ]
- [ ]
- [ ]
- [ ]
- [ ]
- [ ]
- [ ]
- [ ]
- [ ]
- [ ]
- [ ]
- [ ]
- [ ]
- [ ]
- [ ]
- [ ]
- [ ]
- [ ]

Appointments/Dates
- [ ]
- [ ]
- [ ]

Calls/Emails
- [ ]
- [ ]
- [ ]
- [ ]
- [ ]
- [ ]
- [ ]

Today I'm Grateful for:

Ideas/Plans

➡ = Forward   X = Delete   ✓ = Completed

Daily Breakdown:

NOTES

4 AM

5 AM

6 AM

7 AM

8 AM

9 AM

10 AM

11 AM

12 PM

1 PM

2 PM

3 PM

4 PM

5 PM

6 PM

7 PM

8 PM

9 PM

10 PM

Weekly Time Map

Top 3 priorities this week:

Time		Monday	Tuesday	Wednesday
4 a.m.	:00			
	:30			
5 a.m.	:00			
	:30			
6 a.m.	:00			
	:30			
7 a.m.	:00			
	:30			
8 a.m.	:00			
	:30			
9 a.m.	:00			
	:30			
10 a.m.	:00			
	:30			
11 a.m.	:00			
	:30			
12 p.m.	:00			
	:30			
1 p.m.	:00			
	:30			
2 p.m.	:00			
	:30			
3 p.m.	:00			
	:30			
4 p.m.	:00			
	:30			
5 p.m.	:00			
	:30			
6 p.m.	:00			
	:30			
7 p.m.	:00			
	:30			
8 p.m.	:00			
	:30			
9 p.m.	:00			
	:30			
10 p.m.	:00			
	:30			

☐ Thursday	☐ Friday	☐ Saturday	☐ Sunday

Plan the Day to Achieve the Most Important Goals.

Monday

Top 3 Priorities Today:
- [ ]
- [ ]
- [ ]

Hour of Power
- [ ] Prayer / 20 min
- [ ] Read / 20 min
- [ ] Exercise / 20 min

Homework:
- [ ]
- [ ]
- [ ]
- [ ]
- [ ]
- [ ]

To Do:
- [ ]
- [ ]
- [ ]
- [ ]
- [ ]
- [ ]
- [ ]
- [ ]
- [ ]
- [ ]
- [ ]
- [ ]
- [ ]
- [ ]
- [ ]
- [ ]
- [ ]
- [ ]
- [ ]

Appointments/Dates
- [ ]
- [ ]
- [ ]

Calls/Emails
- [ ]
- [ ]
- [ ]
- [ ]
- [ ]
- [ ]
- [ ]

Today I'm Grateful for:

Ideas/Plans

➡ = Forward   X = Delete   ✓ = Completed

Daily Breakdown:

	NOTES
4 AM	
5 AM	
6 AM	
7 AM	
8 AM	
9 AM	
10 AM	
11 AM	
12 PM	
1 PM	
2 PM	
3 PM	
4 PM	
5 PM	
6 PM	
7 PM	
8 PM	
9 PM	
10 PM	

Plan the Day to Achieve the Most Important Goals.

Tuesday

Top 3 Priorities Today:
- ☐
- ☐
- ☐

Hour of Power
- ☐ Prayer / 20 min
- ☐ Read / 20 min
- ☐ Exercise / 20 min

Homework:
- ☐
- ☐
- ☐
- ☐
- ☐
- ☐

To Do:
- ☐
- ☐
- ☐
- ☐
- ☐
- ☐
- ☐
- ☐
- ☐
- ☐
- ☐
- ☐
- ☐
- ☐
- ☐
- ☐
- ☐
- ☐
- ☐
- ☐
- ☐

Appointments/Dates
- ☐
- ☐
- ☐

Calls/Emails
- ☐
- ☐
- ☐
- ☐
- ☐
- ☐
- ☐

Today I'm Grateful for:

Ideas/Plans

➡ = Forward   X = Delete   ✓ = Completed

Daily Breakdown:

4 AM	
5 AM	
6 AM	
7 AM	
8 AM	
9 AM	
10 AM	
11 AM	
12 PM	
1 PM	
2 PM	
3 PM	
4 PM	
5 PM	
6 PM	
7 PM	
8 PM	
9 PM	
10 PM	

NOTES

Plan the Day to Achieve the Most Important Goals.

Wednesday

Top 3 Priorities Today:
- [ ]
- [ ]
- [ ]

Hour of Power
- [ ] Prayer / 20 min
- [ ] Read / 20 min
- [ ] Exercise / 20 min

Homework:
- [ ]
- [ ]
- [ ]
- [ ]
- [ ]
- [ ]

To Do:
- [ ]
- [ ]
- [ ]
- [ ]
- [ ]
- [ ]
- [ ]
- [ ]
- [ ]
- [ ]
- [ ]
- [ ]
- [ ]
- [ ]
- [ ]
- [ ]
- [ ]
- [ ]
- [ ]
- [ ]
- [ ]

Appointments/Dates
- [ ]
- [ ]
- [ ]

Calls/Emails
- [ ]
- [ ]
- [ ]
- [ ]
- [ ]
- [ ]
- [ ]

Today I'm Grateful for:

Ideas/Plans

➡ = Forward   X = Delete   ✓ = Completed

Daily Breakdown:

NOTES

4 AM
5 AM
6 AM
7 AM
8 AM
9 AM
10 AM
11 AM
12 PM
1 PM
2 PM
3 PM
4 PM
5 PM
6 PM
7 PM
8 PM
9 PM
10 PM

Plan the Day to Achieve the Most Important Goals.

Thursday

Top 3 Priorities Today:
- [ ]
- [ ]
- [ ]

Hour of Power
- [ ] Prayer / 20 min
- [ ] Read / 20 min
- [ ] Exercise / 20 min

Homework:
- [ ]
- [ ]
- [ ]
- [ ]
- [ ]
- [ ]

To Do:
- [ ]
- [ ]
- [ ]
- [ ]
- [ ]
- [ ]
- [ ]
- [ ]
- [ ]
- [ ]
- [ ]
- [ ]
- [ ]
- [ ]
- [ ]
- [ ]
- [ ]
- [ ]
- [ ]
- [ ]
- [ ]
- [ ]

Appointments/Dates
- [ ]
- [ ]
- [ ]

Calls/Emails
- [ ]
- [ ]
- [ ]
- [ ]
- [ ]
- [ ]
- [ ]

Today I'm Grateful for:

Ideas/Plans

➡ = Forward   X = Delete   ✓ = Completed

Daily Breakdown:

NOTES

4 AM
5 AM
6 AM
7 AM
8 AM
9 AM
10 AM
11 AM
12 PM
1 PM
2 PM
3 PM
4 PM
5 PM
6 PM
7 PM
8 PM
9 PM
10 PM

Plan the Day to Achieve the Most Important Goals.

Friday

Top 3 Priorities Today:
- [ ]
- [ ]
- [ ]

Hour of Power
- [ ] Prayer / 20 min
- [ ] Read / 20 min
- [ ] Exercise / 20 min

Homework:
- [ ]
- [ ]
- [ ]
- [ ]
- [ ]
- [ ]

To Do:
- [ ]
- [ ]
- [ ]
- [ ]
- [ ]
- [ ]
- [ ]
- [ ]
- [ ]
- [ ]
- [ ]
- [ ]
- [ ]
- [ ]
- [ ]
- [ ]
- [ ]
- [ ]
- [ ]
- [ ]

Appointments/Dates
- [ ]
- [ ]
- [ ]

Calls/Emails
- [ ]
- [ ]
- [ ]
- [ ]
- [ ]
- [ ]
- [ ]

Today I'm Grateful for:

Ideas/Plans

➡ = Forward   X = Delete   ✓ = Completed

Daily Breakdown:

4 AM
5 AM
6 AM
7 AM
8 AM
9 AM
10 AM
11 AM
12 PM
1 PM
2 PM
3 PM
4 PM
5 PM
6 PM
7 PM
8 PM
9 PM
10 PM

NOTES

Weekly Reflections

How do you plan to rest this weekend?

What will you NOT do in order to find rest?

What will you do that is Life-Giving?

List 3 -5 Relationships you want to invest in this weekend:
- [ ]
- [ ]
- [ ]
- [ ]
- [ ]

How will you invest in those relationships?
- [ ]
- [ ]
- [ ]
- [ ]
- [ ]

What have I read/heard this week that stood out?

How will I implement what I learned this week?

What are my 3 Biggest Wins for this week?
- [ ]
- [ ]
- [ ]

What are my top 3 priorities for next week?
- [ ]
- [ ]
- [ ]

| What God has told me to do this year: | What God did for me this week: |

What God is saying Now!

| What am I asking God for this week? | My next Steps to obey what God has said: |

Plan the Day to Achieve the Most Important Goals.

Saturday

Top 3 Priorities Today:
- [ ]
- [ ]
- [ ]

Hour of Power
- [ ] Prayer / 20 min
- [ ] Read / 20 min
- [ ] Exercise / 20 min

Homework:
- [ ]
- [ ]
- [ ]
- [ ]
- [ ]
- [ ]

To Do:
- [ ]
- [ ]
- [ ]
- [ ]
- [ ]
- [ ]
- [ ]
- [ ]
- [ ]
- [ ]
- [ ]
- [ ]
- [ ]
- [ ]
- [ ]
- [ ]
- [ ]
- [ ]
- [ ]
- [ ]
- [ ]
- [ ]

Appointments/Dates
- [ ]
- [ ]
- [ ]

Calls/Emails
- [ ]
- [ ]
- [ ]
- [ ]
- [ ]
- [ ]
- [ ]

Today I'm Grateful for:

Ideas/Plans

➡ = Forward   X = Delete   ✓ = Completed

Daily Breakdown:

	NOTES

4 AM
5 AM
6 AM
7 AM
8 AM
9 AM
10 AM
11 AM
12 PM
1 PM
2 PM
3 PM
4 PM
5 PM
6 PM
7 PM
8 PM
9 PM
10 PM

Plan the Day to Achieve the Most Important Goals.

Sunday

Top 3 Priorities Today:
- [ ]
- [ ]
- [ ]

Hour of Power
- [ ] Prayer / 20 min
- [ ] Read / 20 min
- [ ] Exercise / 20 min

Homework:
- [ ]
- [ ]
- [ ]
- [ ]
- [ ]
- [ ]

To Do:
- [ ]
- [ ]
- [ ]
- [ ]
- [ ]
- [ ]
- [ ]
- [ ]
- [ ]
- [ ]
- [ ]
- [ ]
- [ ]
- [ ]
- [ ]
- [ ]
- [ ]
- [ ]
- [ ]
- [ ]
- [ ]

Appointments/Dates
- [ ]
- [ ]
- [ ]

Calls/Emails
- [ ]
- [ ]
- [ ]
- [ ]
- [ ]
- [ ]
- [ ]

Today I'm Grateful for:

Ideas/Plans

➡ = Forward   X = Delete   ✓ = Completed

Daily Breakdown:

NOTES

4 AM
5 AM
6 AM
7 AM
8 AM
9 AM
10 AM
11 AM
12 PM
1 PM
2 PM
3 PM
4 PM
5 PM
6 PM
7 PM
8 PM
9 PM
10 PM

MONTH

Top 3 priorities this month :

☐
☐
☐

Things to schedule:

☐ Hosting

☐ Mentoring

☐ Team Meeting

☐ Rest

☐ Life-Giving

NOTES

SUNDAY	MONDAY	TUESDAY
Commit your work to the LORD, and your plans will be established. - Proverbs 16:3		☐
☐	☐	☐
☐	☐	☐
☐	☐	☐
☐	☐	☐
☐	☐	☐

WEDNESDAY	THURSDAY	FRIDAY	SATURDAY
☐	☐	☐	☐
☐	☐	☐	☐
☐	☐	☐	☐
☐	☐	☐	☐
☐	☐	☐	☐
☐	☐	☐	☐

Weekly Time Map

Top 3 priorities this week:

Time		Monday	Tuesday	Wednesday
4 a.m.	:00 :30			
5 a.m.	:00 :30			
6 a.m.	:00 :30			
7 a.m.	:00 :30			
8 a.m.	:00 :30			
9 a.m.	:00 :30			
10 a.m.	:00 :30			
11 a.m.	:00 :30			
12 p.m.	:00 :30			
1 p.m.	:00 :30			
2 p.m.	:00 :30			
3 p.m.	:00 :30			
4 p.m.	:00 :30			
5 p.m.	:00 :30			
6 p.m.	:00 :30			
7 p.m.	:00 :30			
8 p.m.	:00 :30			
9 p.m.	:00 :30			
10 p.m.	:00 :30			

Thursday	Friday	Saturday	Sunday

Plan the Day to Achieve the Most Important Goals.

Monday

Top 3 Priorities Today:
- [ ]
- [ ]
- [ ]

Hour of Power
- [ ] Prayer / 20 min
- [ ] Read / 20 min
- [ ] Exercise / 20 min

Homework:
- [ ]
- [ ]
- [ ]
- [ ]
- [ ]
- [ ]

To Do:
- [ ]
- [ ]
- [ ]
- [ ]
- [ ]
- [ ]
- [ ]
- [ ]
- [ ]
- [ ]
- [ ]
- [ ]
- [ ]
- [ ]
- [ ]
- [ ]
- [ ]
- [ ]
- [ ]
- [ ]

Appointments/Dates
- [ ]
- [ ]
- [ ]

Calls/Emails
- [ ]
- [ ]
- [ ]
- [ ]
- [ ]
- [ ]
- [ ]

Today I'm Grateful for:

Ideas/Plans

➡ = Forward   X = Delete   ✓ = Completed

Daily Breakdown:

4 AM
5 AM
6 AM
7 AM
8 AM
9 AM
10 AM
11 AM
12 PM
1 PM
2 PM
3 PM
4 PM
5 PM
6 PM
7 PM
8 PM
9 PM
10 PM

NOTES

Plan the Day to Achieve the Most Important Goals.

Tuesday

Top 3 Priorities Today:
- [ ]
- [ ]
- [ ]

Hour of Power
- [ ] Prayer / 20 min
- [ ] Read / 20 min
- [ ] Exercise / 20 min

Homework:
- [ ]
- [ ]
- [ ]
- [ ]
- [ ]
- [ ]

To Do:
- [ ]
- [ ]
- [ ]
- [ ]
- [ ]
- [ ]
- [ ]
- [ ]
- [ ]
- [ ]
- [ ]
- [ ]
- [ ]
- [ ]
- [ ]
- [ ]
- [ ]
- [ ]
- [ ]
- [ ]

Appointments/Dates
- [ ]
- [ ]
- [ ]

Calls/Emails
- [ ]
- [ ]
- [ ]
- [ ]
- [ ]
- [ ]
- [ ]

Today I'm Grateful for:

Ideas/Plans

➡ = Forward   X = Delete   ✓ = Completed

Daily Breakdown:

4 AM
5 AM
6 AM
7 AM
8 AM
9 AM
10 AM
11 AM
12 PM
1 PM
2 PM
3 PM
4 PM
5 PM
6 PM
7 PM
8 PM
9 PM
10 PM

NOTES

Plan the Day to Achieve the Most Important Goals.

Wednesday

Top 3 Priorities Today:
- [ ]
- [ ]
- [ ]

Hour of Power
- [ ] Prayer / 20 min
- [ ] Read / 20 min
- [ ] Exercise / 20 min

Homework:
- [ ]
- [ ]
- [ ]
- [ ]
- [ ]
- [ ]

To Do:
- [ ]
- [ ]
- [ ]
- [ ]
- [ ]
- [ ]
- [ ]
- [ ]
- [ ]
- [ ]
- [ ]
- [ ]
- [ ]
- [ ]
- [ ]
- [ ]
- [ ]
- [ ]
- [ ]
- [ ]

Appointments/Dates
- [ ]
- [ ]
- [ ]

Calls/Emails
- [ ]
- [ ]
- [ ]
- [ ]
- [ ]
- [ ]
- [ ]

Today I'm Grateful for:

Ideas/Plans

➡ = Forward   X = Delete   ✓ = Completed

Daily Breakdown:

4 AM	
5 AM	
6 AM	
7 AM	
8 AM	
9 AM	
10 AM	
11 AM	
12 PM	
1 PM	
2 PM	
3 PM	
4 PM	
5 PM	
6 PM	
7 PM	
8 PM	
9 PM	
10 PM	

NOTES

Plan the Day to Achieve the Most Important Goals.

Thursday

Top 3 Priorities Today:
- [ ]
- [ ]
- [ ]

Hour of Power
- [ ] Prayer / 20 min
- [ ] Read / 20 min
- [ ] Exercise / 20 min

Homework:
- [ ]
- [ ]
- [ ]
- [ ]
- [ ]
- [ ]

To Do:
- [ ]
- [ ]
- [ ]
- [ ]
- [ ]
- [ ]
- [ ]
- [ ]
- [ ]
- [ ]
- [ ]
- [ ]
- [ ]
- [ ]
- [ ]
- [ ]
- [ ]
- [ ]
- [ ]
- [ ]
- [ ]

Appointments/Dates
- [ ]
- [ ]
- [ ]

Calls/Emails
- [ ]
- [ ]
- [ ]
- [ ]
- [ ]
- [ ]
- [ ]

Today I'm Grateful for:

Ideas/Plans

➡ = Forward   X = Delete   ✓ = Completed

Daily Breakdown:

NOTES

4 AM
5 AM
6 AM
7 AM
8 AM
9 AM
10 AM
11 AM
12 PM
1 PM
2 PM
3 PM
4 PM
5 PM
6 PM
7 PM
8 PM
9 PM
10 PM

Plan the Day to Achieve the Most Important Goals.

Friday

Top 3 Priorities Today:
- [ ]
- [ ]
- [ ]

Hour of Power
- [ ] Prayer / 20 min
- [ ] Read / 20 min
- [ ] Exercise / 20 min

Homework:
- [ ]
- [ ]
- [ ]
- [ ]
- [ ]
- [ ]

To Do:
- [ ]
- [ ]
- [ ]
- [ ]
- [ ]
- [ ]
- [ ]
- [ ]
- [ ]
- [ ]
- [ ]
- [ ]
- [ ]
- [ ]
- [ ]
- [ ]
- [ ]
- [ ]
- [ ]
- [ ]
- [ ]

Appointments/Dates
- [ ]
- [ ]
- [ ]

Calls/Emails
- [ ]
- [ ]
- [ ]
- [ ]
- [ ]
- [ ]
- [ ]

Today I'm Grateful for:

Ideas/Plans

➡ = Forward   X = Delete   ✓ = Completed

Daily Breakdown:

	NOTES

4 AM
5 AM
6 AM
7 AM
8 AM
9 AM
10 AM
11 AM
12 PM
1 PM
2 PM
3 PM
4 PM
5 PM
6 PM
7 PM
8 PM
9 PM
10 PM

Weekly Reflections

How do you plan to rest this weekend?

What will you NOT do in order to find rest?

What will you do that is Life-Giving?

List 3 -5 Relationships you want to invest in this weekend:
- [ ]
- [ ]
- [ ]
- [ ]
- [ ]

How will you invest in those relationships?
- [ ]
- [ ]
- [ ]
- [ ]
- [ ]

What have I read/heard this week that stood out?

How will I implement what I learned this week?

What are my 3 Biggest Wins for this week?
- [ ]
- [ ]
- [ ]

What are my top 3 priorities for next week?
- [ ]
- [ ]
- [ ]

What God has told me to do this year:	What God did for me this week:

What God is saying Now!

What am I asking God for this week?	My next Steps to obey what God has said:

Plan the Day to Achieve the Most Important Goals.		Saturday
Top 3 Priorities Today: ☐ ☐ ☐	Hour of Power ☐ Prayer / 20 min ☐ Read / 20 min ☐ Exercise / 20 min	Homework: ☐ ☐ ☐ ☐ ☐ ☐
To Do: ☐		Appointments/Dates ☐ ☐ ☐
		Calls/Emails ☐ ☐ ☐ ☐ ☐ ☐ ☐
		Today I'm Grateful for:
Ideas/Plans		

➡ = Forward   X = Delete   ✓ = Completed

Daily Breakdown:

NOTES

4 AM
5 AM
6 AM
7 AM
8 AM
9 AM
10 AM
11 AM
12 PM
1 PM
2 PM
3 PM
4 PM
5 PM
6 PM
7 PM
8 PM
9 PM
10 PM

Plan the Day to Achieve the Most Important Goals.	Sunday

Top 3 Priorities Today:
- [ ]
- [ ]
- [ ]

Hour of Power
- [ ] Prayer / 20 min
- [ ] Read / 20 min
- [ ] Exercise / 20 min

Homework:
- [ ]
- [ ]
- [ ]
- [ ]
- [ ]
- [ ]

To Do:
- [ ]
- [ ]
- [ ]
- [ ]
- [ ]
- [ ]
- [ ]
- [ ]
- [ ]
- [ ]
- [ ]
- [ ]
- [ ]
- [ ]
- [ ]
- [ ]
- [ ]
- [ ]
- [ ]
- [ ]
- [ ]

Appointments/Dates
- [ ]
- [ ]
- [ ]

Calls/Emails
- [ ]
- [ ]
- [ ]
- [ ]
- [ ]
- [ ]
- [ ]

Today I'm Grateful for:

Ideas/Plans

➡ = Forward   X = Delete   ✓ = Completed

Daily Breakdown:

	NOTES

4 AM
5 AM
6 AM
7 AM
8 AM
9 AM
10 AM
11 AM
12 PM
1 PM
2 PM
3 PM
4 PM
5 PM
6 PM
7 PM
8 PM
9 PM
10 PM

Weekly Time Map

Top 3 priorities this week:

Time		Monday	Tuesday	Wednesday
4 a.m.	:00			
	:30			
5 a.m.	:00			
	:30			
6 a.m.	:00			
	:30			
7 a.m.	:00			
	:30			
8 a.m.	:00			
	:30			
9 a.m.	:00			
	:30			
10 a.m.	:00			
	:30			
11 a.m.	:00			
	:30			
12 p.m.	:00			
	:30			
1 p.m.	:00			
	:30			
2 p.m.	:00			
	:30			
3 p.m.	:00			
	:30			
4 p.m.	:00			
	:30			
5 p.m.	:00			
	:30			
6 p.m.	:00			
	:30			
7 p.m.	:00			
	:30			
8 p.m.	:00			
	:30			
9 p.m.	:00			
	:30			
10 p.m.	:00			
	:30			

☐ Thursday	☐ Friday	☐ Saturday	☐ Sunday

Plan the Day to Achieve the Most Important Goals.

Monday

Top 3 Priorities Today:
- [ ]
- [ ]
- [ ]

Hour of Power
- [ ] Prayer / 20 min
- [ ] Read / 20 min
- [ ] Exercise / 20 min

Homework:
- [ ]
- [ ]
- [ ]
- [ ]
- [ ]
- [ ]

To Do:
- [ ]
- [ ]
- [ ]
- [ ]
- [ ]
- [ ]
- [ ]
- [ ]
- [ ]
- [ ]
- [ ]
- [ ]
- [ ]
- [ ]
- [ ]
- [ ]
- [ ]
- [ ]
- [ ]
- [ ]
- [ ]

Appointments/Dates
- [ ]
- [ ]
- [ ]

Calls/Emails
- [ ]
- [ ]
- [ ]
- [ ]
- [ ]
- [ ]
- [ ]

Today I'm Grateful for:

Ideas/Plans

➡ = Forward   X = Delete   ✓ = Completed

Daily Breakdown:

NOTES

4 AM
5 AM
6 AM
7 AM
8 AM
9 AM
10 AM
11 AM
12 PM
1 PM
2 PM
3 PM
4 PM
5 PM
6 PM
7 PM
8 PM
9 PM
10 PM

Plan the Day to Achieve the Most Important Goals.

Tuesday

Top 3 Priorities Today:
- [ ]
- [ ]
- [ ]

Hour of Power
- [ ] Prayer / 20 min
- [ ] Read / 20 min
- [ ] Exercise / 20 min

Homework:
- [ ]
- [ ]
- [ ]
- [ ]
- [ ]
- [ ]

To Do:
- [ ]
- [ ]
- [ ]
- [ ]
- [ ]
- [ ]
- [ ]
- [ ]
- [ ]
- [ ]
- [ ]
- [ ]
- [ ]
- [ ]
- [ ]
- [ ]
- [ ]
- [ ]
- [ ]
- [ ]
- [ ]

Appointments/Dates
- [ ]
- [ ]
- [ ]

Calls/Emails
- [ ]
- [ ]
- [ ]
- [ ]
- [ ]
- [ ]
- [ ]

Today I'm Grateful for:

Ideas/Plans

➡ = Forward   X = Delete   ✓ = Completed

Daily Breakdown:

NOTES

4 AM
5 AM
6 AM
7 AM
8 AM
9 AM
10 AM
11 AM
12 PM
1 PM
2 PM
3 PM
4 PM
5 PM
6 PM
7 PM
8 PM
9 PM
10 PM

Plan the Day to Achieve the Most Important Goals.

Wednesday

Top 3 Priorities Today:
- [ ]
- [ ]
- [ ]

Hour of Power
- [ ] Prayer / 20 min
- [ ] Read / 20 min
- [ ] Exercise / 20 min

Homework:
- [ ]
- [ ]
- [ ]
- [ ]
- [ ]
- [ ]

To Do:
- [ ]
- [ ]
- [ ]
- [ ]
- [ ]
- [ ]
- [ ]
- [ ]
- [ ]
- [ ]
- [ ]
- [ ]
- [ ]
- [ ]
- [ ]
- [ ]
- [ ]
- [ ]
- [ ]
- [ ]

Appointments/Dates
- [ ]
- [ ]
- [ ]

Calls/Emails
- [ ]
- [ ]
- [ ]
- [ ]
- [ ]
- [ ]
- [ ]

Today I'm Grateful for:

Ideas/Plans

➡ = Forward   X = Delete   ✓ = Completed

Daily Breakdown:

4 AM	
5 AM	
6 AM	
7 AM	
8 AM	
9 AM	
10 AM	
11 AM	
12 PM	
1 PM	
2 PM	
3 PM	
4 PM	
5 PM	
6 PM	
7 PM	
8 PM	
9 PM	
10 PM	

NOTES

Plan the Day to Achieve the Most Important Goals.

Thursday

Top 3 Priorities Today:
- [ ]
- [ ]
- [ ]

Hour of Power
- [ ] Prayer / 20 min
- [ ] Read / 20 min
- [ ] Exercise / 20 min

Homework:
- [ ]
- [ ]
- [ ]
- [ ]
- [ ]
- [ ]

To Do:
- [ ]
- [ ]
- [ ]
- [ ]
- [ ]
- [ ]
- [ ]
- [ ]
- [ ]
- [ ]
- [ ]
- [ ]
- [ ]
- [ ]
- [ ]
- [ ]
- [ ]
- [ ]
- [ ]
- [ ]

Appointments/Dates
- [ ]
- [ ]
- [ ]

Calls/Emails
- [ ]
- [ ]
- [ ]
- [ ]
- [ ]
- [ ]
- [ ]

Today I'm Grateful for:

Ideas/Plans

➡ = Forward   X = Delete   ✓ = Completed

Daily Breakdown:

	NOTES

4 AM
5 AM
6 AM
7 AM
8 AM
9 AM
10 AM
11 AM
12 PM
1 PM
2 PM
3 PM
4 PM
5 PM
6 PM
7 PM
8 PM
9 PM
10 PM

Plan the Day to Achieve the Most Important Goals.

Friday

Top 3 Priorities Today:
- ☐
- ☐
- ☐

Hour of Power
- ☐ Prayer / 20 min
- ☐ Read / 20 min
- ☐ Exercise / 20 min

Homework:
- ☐
- ☐
- ☐
- ☐
- ☐
- ☐

To Do:
- ☐
- ☐
- ☐
- ☐
- ☐
- ☐
- ☐
- ☐
- ☐
- ☐
- ☐
- ☐
- ☐
- ☐
- ☐
- ☐
- ☐
- ☐
- ☐
- ☐

Appointments/Dates
- ☐
- ☐
- ☐

Calls/Emails
- ☐
- ☐
- ☐
- ☐
- ☐
- ☐
- ☐

Today I'm Grateful for:

Ideas/Plans

➡ = Forward   X = Delete   ✓ = Completed

Daily Breakdown:

4 AM
5 AM
6 AM
7 AM
8 AM
9 AM
10 AM
11 AM
12 PM
1 PM
2 PM
3 PM
4 PM
5 PM
6 PM
7 PM
8 PM
9 PM
10 PM

NOTES

Weekly Reflections

How do you plan to rest this weekend?

What will you NOT do in order to find rest?

What will you do that is Life-Giving?

List 3 -5 Relationships you want to invest in this weekend:
- [ ]
- [ ]
- [ ]
- [ ]
- [ ]

How will you invest in those relationships?
- [ ]
- [ ]
- [ ]
- [ ]
- [ ]

What have I read/heard this week that stood out?

How will I implement what I learned this week?

What are my 3 Biggest Wins for this week?
- [ ]
- [ ]
- [ ]

What are my top 3 priorities for next week?
- [ ]
- [ ]
- [ ]

What God has told me to do this year:	What God did for me this week:

What God is saying Now!

What am I asking God for this week?	My next Steps to obey what God has said:

Plan the Day to Achieve the Most Important Goals.

Saturday

Top 3 Priorities Today:
- [ ]
- [ ]
- [ ]

Hour of Power
- [ ] Prayer / 20 min
- [ ] Read / 20 min
- [ ] Exercise / 20 min

Homework:
- [ ]
- [ ]
- [ ]
- [ ]
- [ ]
- [ ]

To Do:
- [ ]
- [ ]
- [ ]
- [ ]
- [ ]
- [ ]
- [ ]
- [ ]
- [ ]
- [ ]
- [ ]
- [ ]
- [ ]
- [ ]
- [ ]
- [ ]
- [ ]
- [ ]
- [ ]
- [ ]

Appointments/Dates
- [ ]
- [ ]
- [ ]

Calls/Emails
- [ ]
- [ ]
- [ ]
- [ ]
- [ ]
- [ ]
- [ ]

Today I'm Grateful for:

Ideas/Plans

➡ = Forward   X = Delete   ✓ = Completed

Daily Breakdown:

4 AM
5 AM
6 AM
7 AM
8 AM
9 AM
10 AM
11 AM
12 PM
1 PM
2 PM
3 PM
4 PM
5 PM
6 PM
7 PM
8 PM
9 PM
10 PM

NOTES

Plan the Day to Achieve the Most Important Goals.

Sunday

Top 3 Priorities Today:
- [ ]
- [ ]
- [ ]

Hour of Power
- [ ] Prayer / 20 min
- [ ] Read / 20 min
- [ ] Exercise / 20 min

To Do:
- [ ]
- [ ]
- [ ]
- [ ]
- [ ]
- [ ]
- [ ]
- [ ]
- [ ]
- [ ]
- [ ]
- [ ]
- [ ]
- [ ]
- [ ]
- [ ]
- [ ]
- [ ]
- [ ]
- [ ]
- [ ]

Ideas/Plans

Homework:
- [ ]
- [ ]
- [ ]
- [ ]
- [ ]
- [ ]

Appointments/Dates
- [ ]
- [ ]
- [ ]

Calls/Emails
- [ ]
- [ ]
- [ ]
- [ ]
- [ ]
- [ ]
- [ ]

Today I'm Grateful for:

➤ = Forward   X = Delete   ✓ = Completed

Daily Breakdown:

	NOTES

4 AM
5 AM
6 AM
7 AM
8 AM
9 AM
10 AM
11 AM
12 PM
1 PM
2 PM
3 PM
4 PM
5 PM
6 PM
7 PM
8 PM
9 PM
10 PM

Weekly Time Map

Top 3 priorities this week:

Time		Monday	Tuesday	Wednesday
4 a.m.	:00 :30			
5 a.m.	:00 :30			
6 a.m.	:00 :30			
7 a.m.	:00 :30			
8 a.m.	:00 :30			
9 a.m.	:00 :30			
10 a.m.	:00 :30			
11 a.m.	:00 :30			
12 p.m.	:00 :30			
1 p.m.	:00 :30			
2 p.m.	:00 :30			
3 p.m.	:00 :30			
4 p.m.	:00 :30			
5 p.m.	:00 :30			
6 p.m.	:00 :30			
7 p.m.	:00 :30			
8 p.m.	:00 :30			
9 p.m.	:00 :30			
10 p.m.	:00 :30			

☐ Thursday	☐ Friday	☐ Saturday	Sunday

Plan the Day to Achieve the Most Important Goals.		Monday
Top 3 Priorities Today: ☐ ☐ ☐	**Hour of Power** ☐ Prayer / 20 min ☐ Read / 20 min ☐ Exercise / 20 min	**Homework:** ☐ ☐ ☐ ☐ ☐ ☐
To Do: ☐ ☐ ☐ ☐ ☐ ☐ ☐ ☐ ☐ ☐ ☐ ☐ ☐ ☐ ☐ ☐ ☐ ☐ ☐		**Appointments/Dates** ☐ ☐ ☐
		Calls/Emails ☐ ☐ ☐ ☐ ☐ ☐ ☐
		Today I'm Grateful for:
Ideas/Plans		

➡ = Forward   X = Delete   ✓ = Completed

Daily Breakdown:

NOTES

4 AM
5 AM
6 AM
7 AM
8 AM
9 AM
10 AM
11 AM
12 PM
1 PM
2 PM
3 PM
4 PM
5 PM
6 PM
7 PM
8 PM
9 PM
10 PM

Plan the Day to Achieve the Most Important Goals.

Tuesday

Top 3 Priorities Today:
- [ ]
- [ ]
- [ ]

Hour of Power
- [ ] Prayer / 20 min
- [ ] Read / 20 min
- [ ] Exercise / 20 min

Homework:
- [ ]
- [ ]
- [ ]
- [ ]
- [ ]
- [ ]

To Do:
- [ ]
- [ ]
- [ ]
- [ ]
- [ ]
- [ ]
- [ ]
- [ ]
- [ ]
- [ ]
- [ ]
- [ ]
- [ ]
- [ ]
- [ ]
- [ ]
- [ ]
- [ ]
- [ ]
- [ ]

Appointments/Dates
- [ ]
- [ ]
- [ ]

Calls/Emails
- [ ]
- [ ]
- [ ]
- [ ]
- [ ]
- [ ]
- [ ]

Today I'm Grateful for:

Ideas/Plans

➡ = Forward   X = Delete   ✓ = Completed

Daily Breakdown:

NOTES

4 AM

5 AM

6 AM

7 AM

8 AM

9 AM

10 AM

11 AM

12 PM

1 PM

2 PM

3 PM

4 PM

5 PM

6 PM

7 PM

8 PM

9 PM

10 PM

Plan the Day to Achieve the Most Important Goals.

Wednesday

Top 3 Priorities Today:
- [ ]
- [ ]
- [ ]

Hour of Power
- [ ] Prayer / 20 min
- [ ] Read / 20 min
- [ ] Exercise / 20 min

Homework:
- [ ]
- [ ]
- [ ]
- [ ]
- [ ]
- [ ]

To Do:
- [ ]
- [ ]
- [ ]
- [ ]
- [ ]
- [ ]
- [ ]
- [ ]
- [ ]
- [ ]
- [ ]
- [ ]
- [ ]
- [ ]
- [ ]
- [ ]
- [ ]
- [ ]
- [ ]
- [ ]
- [ ]

Appointments/Dates
- [ ]
- [ ]
- [ ]

Calls/Emails
- [ ]
- [ ]
- [ ]
- [ ]
- [ ]
- [ ]
- [ ]

Today I'm Grateful for:

Ideas/Plans

➡ = Forward   X = Delete   ✓ = Completed

Daily Breakdown:

NOTES

4 AM
5 AM
6 AM
7 AM
8 AM
9 AM
10 AM
11 AM
12 PM
1 PM
2 PM
3 PM
4 PM
5 PM
6 PM
7 PM
8 PM
9 PM
10 PM

Plan the Day to Achieve the Most Important Goals.

Thursday

Top 3 Priorities Today:
- [ ]
- [ ]
- [ ]

Hour of Power
- [ ] Prayer / 20 min
- [ ] Read / 20 min
- [ ] Exercise / 20 min

Homework:
- [ ]
- [ ]
- [ ]
- [ ]
- [ ]
- [ ]

To Do:
- [ ]
- [ ]
- [ ]
- [ ]
- [ ]
- [ ]
- [ ]
- [ ]
- [ ]
- [ ]
- [ ]
- [ ]
- [ ]
- [ ]
- [ ]
- [ ]
- [ ]
- [ ]
- [ ]
- [ ]
- [ ]
- [ ]

Appointments/Dates
- [ ]
- [ ]
- [ ]

Calls/Emails
- [ ]
- [ ]
- [ ]
- [ ]
- [ ]
- [ ]
- [ ]

Today I'm Grateful for:

Ideas/Plans

➡ = Forward   X = Delete   ✓ = Completed

Daily Breakdown:

NOTES

4 AM
5 AM
6 AM
7 AM
8 AM
9 AM
10 AM
11 AM
12 PM
1 PM
2 PM
3 PM
4 PM
5 PM
6 PM
7 PM
8 PM
9 PM
10 PM

Plan the Day to Achieve the Most Important Goals.

Friday

Top 3 Priorities Today:
- [ ]
- [ ]
- [ ]

Hour of Power
- [ ] Prayer / 20 min
- [ ] Read / 20 min
- [ ] Exercise / 20 min

Homework:
- [ ]
- [ ]
- [ ]
- [ ]
- [ ]
- [ ]

To Do:
- [ ]
- [ ]
- [ ]
- [ ]
- [ ]
- [ ]
- [ ]
- [ ]
- [ ]
- [ ]
- [ ]
- [ ]
- [ ]
- [ ]
- [ ]
- [ ]
- [ ]
- [ ]
- [ ]
- [ ]
- [ ]

Appointments/Dates
- [ ]
- [ ]
- [ ]

Calls/Emails
- [ ]
- [ ]
- [ ]
- [ ]
- [ ]
- [ ]
- [ ]

Today I'm Grateful for:

Ideas/Plans

➡ = Forward   X = Delete   ✓ = Completed

Daily Breakdown:

4 AM
5 AM
6 AM
7 AM
8 AM
9 AM
10 AM
11 AM
12 PM
1 PM
2 PM
3 PM
4 PM
5 PM
6 PM
7 PM
8 PM
9 PM
10 PM

NOTES

Weekly Reflections

How do you plan to rest this weekend?

What will you NOT do in order to find rest?

What will you do that is Life-Giving?

List 3 -5 Relationships you want to invest in this weekend:
- [ ]
- [ ]
- [ ]
- [ ]
- [ ]

How will you invest in those relationships?
- [ ]
- [ ]
- [ ]
- [ ]
- [ ]

What have I read/heard this week that stood out?

How will I implement what I learned this week?

What are my 3 Biggest Wins for this week?
- [ ]
- [ ]
- [ ]

What are my top 3 priorities for next week?
- [ ]
- [ ]
- [ ]

What God has told me to do this year:	What God did for me this week:

What God is saying Now!

What am I asking God for this week?	My next Steps to obey what God has said:

Plan the Day to Achieve the Most Important Goals.

Saturday

Top 3 Priorities Today:
- [ ]
- [ ]
- [ ]

Hour of Power
- [ ] Prayer / 20 min
- [ ] Read / 20 min
- [ ] Exercise / 20 min

Homework:
- [ ]
- [ ]
- [ ]
- [ ]
- [ ]
- [ ]

To Do:
- [ ]
- [ ]
- [ ]
- [ ]
- [ ]
- [ ]
- [ ]
- [ ]
- [ ]
- [ ]
- [ ]
- [ ]
- [ ]
- [ ]
- [ ]
- [ ]
- [ ]
- [ ]
- [ ]
- [ ]

Appointments/Dates
- [ ]
- [ ]
- [ ]

Calls/Emails
- [ ]
- [ ]
- [ ]
- [ ]
- [ ]
- [ ]
- [ ]

Today I'm Grateful for:

Ideas/Plans

➡ = Forward   X = Delete   ✓ = Completed

Daily Breakdown:

NOTES

4 AM
5 AM
6 AM
7 AM
8 AM
9 AM
10 AM
11 AM
12 PM
1 PM
2 PM
3 PM
4 PM
5 PM
6 PM
7 PM
8 PM
9 PM
10 PM

Plan the Day to Achieve the Most Important Goals.

Sunday

Top 3 Priorities Today:
- [ ]
- [ ]
- [ ]

Hour of Power
- [ ] Prayer / 20 min
- [ ] Read / 20 min
- [ ] Exercise / 20 min

Homework:
- [ ]
- [ ]
- [ ]
- [ ]
- [ ]
- [ ]

To Do:
- [ ]
- [ ]
- [ ]
- [ ]
- [ ]
- [ ]
- [ ]
- [ ]
- [ ]
- [ ]
- [ ]
- [ ]
- [ ]
- [ ]
- [ ]
- [ ]
- [ ]
- [ ]
- [ ]
- [ ]

Appointments/Dates
- [ ]
- [ ]
- [ ]

Calls/Emails
- [ ]
- [ ]
- [ ]
- [ ]
- [ ]
- [ ]
- [ ]

Today I'm Grateful for:

Ideas/Plans

➡ = Forward   X = Delete   ✓ = Completed

Daily Breakdown:

NOTES

4 AM
5 AM
6 AM
7 AM
8 AM
9 AM
10 AM
11 AM
12 PM
1 PM
2 PM
3 PM
4 PM
5 PM
6 PM
7 PM
8 PM
9 PM
10 PM

Weekly Time Map

Top 3 priorities this week:

Time		Monday	Tuesday	Wednesday
4 a.m.	:00			
	:30			
5 a.m.	:00			
	:30			
6 a.m.	:00			
	:30			
7 a.m.	:00			
	:30			
8 a.m.	:00			
	:30			
9 a.m.	:00			
	:30			
10 a.m.	:00			
	:30			
11 a.m.	:00			
	:30			
12 p.m.	:00			
	:30			
1 p.m.	:00			
	:30			
2 p.m.	:00			
	:30			
3 p.m.	:00			
	:30			
4 p.m.	:00			
	:30			
5 p.m.	:00			
	:30			
6 p.m.	:00			
	:30			
7 p.m.	:00			
	:30			
8 p.m.	:00			
	:30			
9 p.m.	:00			
	:30			
10 p.m.	:00			
	:30			

☐	☐	☐	
Thursday	Friday	Saturday	Sunday

Plan the Day to Achieve the Most Important Goals.		Monday
Top 3 Priorities Today: ☐ ☐ ☐	Hour of Power ☐ Prayer / 20 min ☐ Read / 20 min ☐ Exercise / 20 min	Homework: ☐ ☐ ☐ ☐ ☐
To Do: ☐ ☐ ☐ ☐ ☐ ☐ ☐ ☐ ☐ ☐ ☐ ☐ ☐ ☐ ☐ ☐ ☐ ☐ ☐		Appointments/Dates ☐ ☐ ☐
		Calls/Emails ☐ ☐ ☐ ☐ ☐ ☐ ☐
Ideas/Plans		Today I'm Grateful for:

➡ = Forward   X = Delete   ✓ = Completed

Daily Breakdown:

NOTES

4 AM
5 AM
6 AM
7 AM
8 AM
9 AM
10 AM
11 AM
12 PM
1 PM
2 PM
3 PM
4 PM
5 PM
6 PM
7 PM
8 PM
9 PM
10 PM

Plan the Day to Achieve the Most Important Goals.

Tuesday

Top 3 Priorities Today:	Hour of Power
☐	☐ Prayer / 20 min
☐	☐ Read / 20 min
☐	☐ Exercise / 20 min

Homework:
- ☐
- ☐
- ☐
- ☐
- ☐
- ☐

To Do:
- ☐
- ☐
- ☐
- ☐
- ☐
- ☐
- ☐
- ☐
- ☐
- ☐
- ☐
- ☐
- ☐
- ☐
- ☐
- ☐
- ☐
- ☐
- ☐
- ☐

Appointments/Dates
- ☐
- ☐
- ☐

Calls/Emails
- ☐
- ☐
- ☐
- ☐
- ☐
- ☐
- ☐

Today I'm Grateful for:

Ideas/Plans

➡ = Forward   X = Delete   ✓ = Completed

Daily Breakdown:

4 AM	
5 AM	
6 AM	
7 AM	
8 AM	
9 AM	
10 AM	
11 AM	
12 PM	
1 PM	
2 PM	
3 PM	
4 PM	
5 PM	
6 PM	
7 PM	
8 PM	
9 PM	
10 PM	

NOTES

Plan the Day to Achieve the Most Important Goals.

Wednesday

Top 3 Priorities Today:
- ☐
- ☐
- ☐

Hour of Power
- ☐ Prayer / 20 min
- ☐ Read / 20 min
- ☐ Exercise / 20 min

Homework:
- ☐
- ☐
- ☐
- ☐
- ☐
- ☐

To Do:
- ☐
- ☐
- ☐
- ☐
- ☐
- ☐
- ☐
- ☐
- ☐
- ☐
- ☐
- ☐
- ☐
- ☐
- ☐
- ☐
- ☐
- ☐
- ☐
- ☐
- ☐
- ☐
- ☐
- ☐

Appointments/Dates
- ☐
- ☐
- ☐

Calls/Emails
- ☐
- ☐
- ☐
- ☐
- ☐
- ☐
- ☐

Today I'm Grateful for:

Ideas/Plans

➡ = Forward   X = Delete   ✓ = Completed

Daily Breakdown:

	NOTES

4 AM
5 AM
6 AM
7 AM
8 AM
9 AM
10 AM
11 AM
12 PM
1 PM
2 PM
3 PM
4 PM
5 PM
6 PM
7 PM
8 PM
9 PM
10 PM

Plan the Day to Achieve the Most Important Goals.

Thursday

Top 3 Priorities Today:
- [ ]
- [ ]
- [ ]

Hour of Power
- [ ] Prayer / 20 min
- [ ] Read / 20 min
- [ ] Exercise / 20 min

Homework:
- [ ]
- [ ]
- [ ]
- [ ]
- [ ]
- [ ]

To Do:
- [ ]
- [ ]
- [ ]
- [ ]
- [ ]
- [ ]
- [ ]
- [ ]
- [ ]
- [ ]
- [ ]
- [ ]
- [ ]
- [ ]
- [ ]
- [ ]
- [ ]
- [ ]
- [ ]
- [ ]

Appointments/Dates
- [ ]
- [ ]
- [ ]

Calls/Emails
- [ ]
- [ ]
- [ ]
- [ ]
- [ ]
- [ ]
- [ ]

Today I'm Grateful for:

Ideas/Plans

➡ = Forward   X = Delete   ✓ = Completed

Daily Breakdown:

	NOTES

4 AM
5 AM
6 AM
7 AM
8 AM
9 AM
10 AM
11 AM
12 PM
1 PM
2 PM
3 PM
4 PM
5 PM
6 PM
7 PM
8 PM
9 PM
10 PM

Plan the Day to Achieve the Most Important Goals.

Friday

Top 3 Priorities Today:
- [ ]
- [ ]
- [ ]

Hour of Power
- [ ] Prayer / 20 min
- [ ] Read / 20 min
- [ ] Exercise / 20 min

Homework:
- [ ]
- [ ]
- [ ]
- [ ]
- [ ]
- [ ]

To Do:
- [ ]
- [ ]
- [ ]
- [ ]
- [ ]
- [ ]
- [ ]
- [ ]
- [ ]
- [ ]
- [ ]
- [ ]
- [ ]
- [ ]
- [ ]
- [ ]
- [ ]
- [ ]
- [ ]
- [ ]

Appointments/Dates
- [ ]
- [ ]
- [ ]

Calls/Emails
- [ ]
- [ ]
- [ ]
- [ ]
- [ ]
- [ ]
- [ ]

Today I'm Grateful for:

Ideas/Plans

➡ = Forward   X = Delete   ✓ = Completed

Daily Breakdown:

4 AM
5 AM
6 AM
7 AM
8 AM
9 AM
10 AM
11 AM
12 PM
1 PM
2 PM
3 PM
4 PM
5 PM
6 PM
7 PM
8 PM
9 PM
10 PM

NOTES

Weekly Reflections

How do you plan to rest this weekend?

What will you NOT do in order to find rest?

What will you do that is Life-Giving?

List 3 -5 Relationships you want to invest in this weekend:
- [ ]
- [ ]
- [ ]
- [ ]
- [ ]

How will you invest in those relationships?
- [ ]
- [ ]
- [ ]
- [ ]
- [ ]

What have I read/heard this week that stood out?

How will I implement what I learned this week?

What are my 3 Biggest Wins for this week?
- [ ]
- [ ]
- [ ]

What are my top 3 priorities for next week?
- [ ]
- [ ]
- [ ]

What God has told me to do this year:	What God did for me this week:

What God is saying Now!

What am I asking God for this week?	My next Steps to obey what God has said:

Plan the Day to Achieve the Most Important Goals.

Saturday

Top 3 Priorities Today:
- [ ]
- [ ]
- [ ]

Hour of Power
- [ ] Prayer / 20 min
- [ ] Read / 20 min
- [ ] Exercise / 20 min

Homework:
- [ ]
- [ ]
- [ ]
- [ ]
- [ ]
- [ ]

To Do:
- [ ]
- [ ]
- [ ]
- [ ]
- [ ]
- [ ]
- [ ]
- [ ]
- [ ]
- [ ]
- [ ]
- [ ]
- [ ]
- [ ]
- [ ]
- [ ]
- [ ]
- [ ]
- [ ]
- [ ]
- [ ]

Appointments/Dates
- [ ]
- [ ]
- [ ]

Calls/Emails
- [ ]
- [ ]
- [ ]
- [ ]
- [ ]
- [ ]
- [ ]

Today I'm Grateful for:

Ideas/Plans

➡ = Forward   X = Delete   ✓ = Completed

Daily Breakdown:

NOTES

4 AM

5 AM

6 AM

7 AM

8 AM

9 AM

10 AM

11 AM

12 PM

1 PM

2 PM

3 PM

4 PM

5 PM

6 PM

7 PM

8 PM

9 PM

10 PM

Plan the Day to Achieve the Most Important Goals.

Sunday

Top 3 Priorities Today:
- [ ]
- [ ]
- [ ]

Hour of Power
- [ ] Prayer / 20 min
- [ ] Read / 20 min
- [ ] Exercise / 20 min

Homework:
- [ ]
- [ ]
- [ ]
- [ ]
- [ ]
- [ ]

To Do:
- [ ]
- [ ]
- [ ]
- [ ]
- [ ]
- [ ]
- [ ]
- [ ]
- [ ]
- [ ]
- [ ]
- [ ]
- [ ]
- [ ]
- [ ]
- [ ]
- [ ]
- [ ]
- [ ]
- [ ]
- [ ]
- [ ]

Appointments/Dates
- [ ]
- [ ]
- [ ]

Calls/Emails
- [ ]
- [ ]
- [ ]
- [ ]
- [ ]
- [ ]
- [ ]

Today I'm Grateful for:

Ideas/Plans

➡ = Forward   X = Delete   ✓ = Completed

Daily Breakdown:

NOTES

4 AM

5 AM

6 AM

7 AM

8 AM

9 AM

10 AM

11 AM

12 PM

1 PM

2 PM

3 PM

4 PM

5 PM

6 PM

7 PM

8 PM

9 PM

10 PM

Weekly Time Map

Top 3 priorities this week:

Time		Monday	Tuesday	Wednesday
4 a.m.	:00			
	:30			
5 a.m.	:00			
	:30			
6 a.m.	:00			
	:30			
7 a.m.	:00			
	:30			
8 a.m.	:00			
	:30			
9 a.m.	:00			
	:30			
10 a.m.	:00			
	:30			
11 a.m.	:00			
	:30			
12 p.m.	:00			
	:30			
1 p.m.	:00			
	:30			
2 p.m.	:00			
	:30			
3 p.m.	:00			
	:30			
4 p.m.	:00			
	:30			
5 p.m.	:00			
	:30			
6 p.m.	:00			
	:30			
7 p.m.	:00			
	:30			
8 p.m.	:00			
	:30			
9 p.m.	:00			
	:30			
10 p.m.	:00			
	:30			

☐ Thursday	☐ Friday	☐ Saturday	☐ Sunday

Plan the Day to Achieve the Most Important Goals.

Monday

Top 3 Priorities Today:
- [ ]
- [ ]
- [ ]

Hour of Power
- [ ] Prayer / 20 min
- [ ] Read / 20 min
- [ ] Exercise / 20 min

Homework:
- [ ]
- [ ]
- [ ]
- [ ]
- [ ]
- [ ]

To Do:
- [ ]
- [ ]
- [ ]
- [ ]
- [ ]
- [ ]
- [ ]
- [ ]
- [ ]
- [ ]
- [ ]
- [ ]
- [ ]
- [ ]
- [ ]
- [ ]
- [ ]
- [ ]
- [ ]
- [ ]

Appointments/Dates
- [ ]
- [ ]
- [ ]

Calls/Emails
- [ ]
- [ ]
- [ ]
- [ ]
- [ ]
- [ ]
- [ ]

Today I'm Grateful for:

Ideas/Plans

➡ = Forward   X = Delete   ✓ = Completed

Daily Breakdown:

NOTES

4 AM
5 AM
6 AM
7 AM
8 AM
9 AM
10 AM
11 AM
12 PM
1 PM
2 PM
3 PM
4 PM
5 PM
6 PM
7 PM
8 PM
9 PM
10 PM

Plan the Day to Achieve the Most Important Goals.

Tuesday

Top 3 Priorities Today:
- [ ]
- [ ]
- [ ]

Hour of Power
- [ ] Prayer / 20 min
- [ ] Read / 20 min
- [ ] Exercise / 20 min

Homework:
- [ ]
- [ ]
- [ ]
- [ ]
- [ ]
- [ ]

To Do:
- [ ]
- [ ]
- [ ]
- [ ]
- [ ]
- [ ]
- [ ]
- [ ]
- [ ]
- [ ]
- [ ]
- [ ]
- [ ]
- [ ]
- [ ]
- [ ]
- [ ]
- [ ]
- [ ]
- [ ]
- [ ]
- [ ]

Appointments/Dates
- [ ]
- [ ]
- [ ]

Calls/Emails
- [ ]
- [ ]
- [ ]
- [ ]
- [ ]
- [ ]
- [ ]

Today I'm Grateful for:

Ideas/Plans

➡ = Forward   X = Delete   ✓ = Completed

Daily Breakdown:

4 AM	
5 AM	
6 AM	
7 AM	
8 AM	
9 AM	
10 AM	
11 AM	
12 PM	
1 PM	
2 PM	
3 PM	
4 PM	
5 PM	
6 PM	
7 PM	
8 PM	
9 PM	
10 PM	

NOTES

Plan the Day to Achieve the Most Important Goals.

Wednesday

Top 3 Priorities Today:
- [ ]
- [ ]
- [ ]

Hour of Power
- [ ] Prayer / 20 min
- [ ] Read / 20 min
- [ ] Exercise / 20 min

Homework:
- [ ]
- [ ]
- [ ]
- [ ]
- [ ]
- [ ]

To Do:
- [ ]
- [ ]
- [ ]
- [ ]
- [ ]
- [ ]
- [ ]
- [ ]
- [ ]
- [ ]
- [ ]
- [ ]
- [ ]
- [ ]
- [ ]
- [ ]
- [ ]
- [ ]
- [ ]
- [ ]

Appointments/Dates
- [ ]
- [ ]
- [ ]

Calls/Emails
- [ ]
- [ ]
- [ ]
- [ ]
- [ ]
- [ ]
- [ ]

Today I'm Grateful for:

Ideas/Plans

➡ = Forward   X = Delete   ✓ = Completed

Daily Breakdown:

NOTES

4 AM
5 AM
6 AM
7 AM
8 AM
9 AM
10 AM
11 AM
12 PM
1 PM
2 PM
3 PM
4 PM
5 PM
6 PM
7 PM
8 PM
9 PM
10 PM

Plan the Day to Achieve the Most Important Goals.

Thursday

Top 3 Priorities Today:
- [ ]
- [ ]
- [ ]

Hour of Power
- [ ] Prayer / 20 min
- [ ] Read / 20 min
- [ ] Exercise / 20 min

Homework:
- [ ]
- [ ]
- [ ]
- [ ]
- [ ]
- [ ]

To Do:
- [ ]
- [ ]
- [ ]
- [ ]
- [ ]
- [ ]
- [ ]
- [ ]
- [ ]
- [ ]
- [ ]
- [ ]
- [ ]
- [ ]
- [ ]
- [ ]
- [ ]
- [ ]
- [ ]
- [ ]
- [ ]

Appointments/Dates
- [ ]
- [ ]
- [ ]

Calls/Emails
- [ ]
- [ ]
- [ ]
- [ ]
- [ ]
- [ ]
- [ ]

Today I'm Grateful for:

Ideas/Plans

➡ = Forward   X = Delete   ✓ = Completed

Daily Breakdown:

NOTES

4 AM
5 AM
6 AM
7 AM
8 AM
9 AM
10 AM
11 AM
12 PM
1 PM
2 PM
3 PM
4 PM
5 PM
6 PM
7 PM
8 PM
9 PM
10 PM

Plan the Day to Achieve the Most Important Goals.

Friday

Top 3 Priorities Today:
- [ ]
- [ ]
- [ ]

Hour of Power
- [ ] Prayer / 20 min
- [ ] Read / 20 min
- [ ] Exercise / 20 min

Homework:
- [ ]
- [ ]
- [ ]
- [ ]
- [ ]

To Do:
- [ ]
- [ ]
- [ ]
- [ ]
- [ ]
- [ ]
- [ ]
- [ ]
- [ ]
- [ ]
- [ ]
- [ ]
- [ ]
- [ ]
- [ ]
- [ ]
- [ ]
- [ ]
- [ ]
- [ ]
- [ ]

Appointments/Dates
- [ ]
- [ ]
- [ ]

Calls/Emails
- [ ]
- [ ]
- [ ]
- [ ]
- [ ]
- [ ]
- [ ]

Today I'm Grateful for:

Ideas/Plans

➡ = Forward   X = Delete   ✓ = Completed

Daily Breakdown:

NOTES

4 AM
5 AM
6 AM
7 AM
8 AM
9 AM
10 AM
11 AM
12 PM
1 PM
2 PM
3 PM
4 PM
5 PM
6 PM
7 PM
8 PM
9 PM
10 PM

Weekly Reflections

How do you plan to rest this weekend?

What will you NOT do in order to find rest?

What will you do that is Life-Giving?

List 3 -5 Relationships you want to invest in this weekend:
- [ ]
- [ ]
- [ ]
- [ ]
- [ ]

How will you invest in those relationships?
- [ ]
- [ ]
- [ ]
- [ ]
- [ ]

What have I read/heard this week that stood out?

How will I implement what I learned this week?

What are my 3 Biggest Wins for this week?
- [ ]
- [ ]
- [ ]

What are my top 3 priorities for next week?
- [ ]
- [ ]
- [ ]

What God has told me to do this year:	What God did for me this week:

What God is saying Now!

What am I asking God for this week?	My next Steps to obey what God has said:

Plan the Day to Achieve the Most Important Goals.

Saturday

Top 3 Priorities Today:
- [ ]
- [ ]
- [ ]

Hour of Power
- [ ] Prayer / 20 min
- [ ] Read / 20 min
- [ ] Exercise / 20 min

Homework:
- [ ]
- [ ]
- [ ]
- [ ]
- [ ]
- [ ]

To Do:
- [ ]
- [ ]
- [ ]
- [ ]
- [ ]
- [ ]
- [ ]
- [ ]
- [ ]
- [ ]
- [ ]
- [ ]
- [ ]
- [ ]
- [ ]
- [ ]
- [ ]
- [ ]
- [ ]
- [ ]
- [ ]

Appointments/Dates
- [ ]
- [ ]
- [ ]

Calls/Emails
- [ ]
- [ ]
- [ ]
- [ ]
- [ ]
- [ ]
- [ ]

Today I'm Grateful for:

Ideas/Plans

➡ = Forward   X = Delete   ✓ = Completed

Daily Breakdown:

NOTES

4 AM
5 AM
6 AM
7 AM
8 AM
9 AM
10 AM
11 AM
12 PM
1 PM
2 PM
3 PM
4 PM
5 PM
6 PM
7 PM
8 PM
9 PM
10 PM

Plan the Day to Achieve the Most Important Goals.

Sunday

Top 3 Priorities Today:
- [ ]
- [ ]
- [ ]

Hour of Power
- [ ] Prayer / 20 min
- [ ] Read / 20 min
- [ ] Exercise / 20 min

Homework:
- [ ]
- [ ]
- [ ]
- [ ]
- [ ]
- [ ]

To Do:
- [ ]
- [ ]
- [ ]
- [ ]
- [ ]
- [ ]
- [ ]
- [ ]
- [ ]
- [ ]
- [ ]
- [ ]
- [ ]
- [ ]
- [ ]
- [ ]
- [ ]
- [ ]
- [ ]
- [ ]
- [ ]
- [ ]

Appointments/Dates
- [ ]
- [ ]
- [ ]

Calls/Emails
- [ ]
- [ ]
- [ ]
- [ ]
- [ ]
- [ ]
- [ ]

Today I'm Grateful for:

Ideas/Plans

➡ = Forward   X = Delete   ✓ = Completed

Daily Breakdown:

4 AM
5 AM
6 AM
7 AM
8 AM
9 AM
10 AM
11 AM
12 PM
1 PM
2 PM
3 PM
4 PM
5 PM
6 PM
7 PM
8 PM
9 PM
10 PM

NOTES

MONTH

Top 3 priorities this month :
- [ ]
- [ ]
- [ ]

Things to schedule:
- [ ] Hosting

- [ ] Mentoring

- [ ] Team Meeting

- [ ] Rest

- [ ] Life-Giving

NOTES

SUNDAY	MONDAY	TUESDAY
Delight yourself in the LORD, and he will give you the desires of your heart. - Psalms 37:4		

WEDNESDAY	THURSDAY	FRIDAY	SATURDAY

Weekly Time Map

Top 3 priorities this week:

Time		Monday	Tuesday	Wednesday
4 a.m.	:00			
	:30			
5 a.m.	:00			
	:30			
6 a.m.	:00			
	:30			
7 a.m.	:00			
	:30			
8 a.m.	:00			
	:30			
9 a.m.	:00			
	:30			
10 a.m.	:00			
	:30			
11 a.m.	:00			
	:30			
12 p.m.	:00			
	:30			
1 p.m.	:00			
	:30			
2 p.m.	:00			
	:30			
3 p.m.	:00			
	:30			
4 p.m.	:00			
	:30			
5 p.m.	:00			
	:30			
6 p.m.	:00			
	:30			
7 p.m.	:00			
	:30			
8 p.m.	:00			
	:30			
9 p.m.	:00			
	:30			
10 p.m.	:00			
	:30			

Thursday	Friday	Saturday	Sunday

Plan the Day to Achieve the Most Important Goals.

Monday

Top 3 Priorities Today:
- ☐
- ☐
- ☐

Hour of Power
- ☐ Prayer / 20 min
- ☐ Read / 20 min
- ☐ Exercise / 20 min

Homework:
- ☐
- ☐
- ☐
- ☐
- ☐
- ☐

To Do:
- ☐
- ☐
- ☐
- ☐
- ☐
- ☐
- ☐
- ☐
- ☐
- ☐
- ☐
- ☐
- ☐
- ☐
- ☐
- ☐
- ☐
- ☐
- ☐
- ☐
- ☐

Appointments/Dates
- ☐
- ☐
- ☐

Calls/Emails
- ☐
- ☐
- ☐
- ☐
- ☐
- ☐
- ☐

Today I'm Grateful for:

Ideas/Plans

➡ = Forward   X = Delete   ✓ = Completed

Daily Breakdown:

NOTES

4 AM
5 AM
6 AM
7 AM
8 AM
9 AM
10 AM
11 AM
12 PM
1 PM
2 PM
3 PM
4 PM
5 PM
6 PM
7 PM
8 PM
9 PM
10 PM

Plan the Day to Achieve the Most Important Goals.

Tuesday

Top 3 Priorities Today:
- [ ]
- [ ]
- [ ]

Hour of Power
- [ ] Prayer / 20 min
- [ ] Read / 20 min
- [ ] Exercise / 20 min

Homework:
- [ ]
- [ ]
- [ ]
- [ ]
- [ ]
- [ ]

To Do:
- [ ]
- [ ]
- [ ]
- [ ]
- [ ]
- [ ]
- [ ]
- [ ]
- [ ]
- [ ]
- [ ]
- [ ]
- [ ]
- [ ]
- [ ]
- [ ]
- [ ]
- [ ]
- [ ]
- [ ]

Appointments/Dates
- [ ]
- [ ]
- [ ]

Calls/Emails
- [ ]
- [ ]
- [ ]
- [ ]
- [ ]
- [ ]
- [ ]

Today I'm Grateful for:

Ideas/Plans

➡ = Forward   X = Delete   ✓ = Completed

Daily Breakdown:

NOTES

4 AM

5 AM

6 AM

7 AM

8 AM

9 AM

10 AM

11 AM

12 PM

1 PM

2 PM

3 PM

4 PM

5 PM

6 PM

7 PM

8 PM

9 PM

10 PM

Plan the Day to Achieve the Most Important Goals.

Wednesday

Top 3 Priorities Today:
- [ ]
- [ ]
- [ ]

Hour of Power
- [ ] Prayer / 20 min
- [ ] Read / 20 min
- [ ] Exercise / 20 min

Homework:
- [ ]
- [ ]
- [ ]
- [ ]
- [ ]
- [ ]

To Do:
- [ ]
- [ ]
- [ ]
- [ ]
- [ ]
- [ ]
- [ ]
- [ ]
- [ ]
- [ ]
- [ ]
- [ ]
- [ ]
- [ ]
- [ ]
- [ ]
- [ ]
- [ ]
- [ ]

Appointments/Dates
- [ ]
- [ ]
- [ ]

Calls/Emails
- [ ]
- [ ]
- [ ]
- [ ]
- [ ]
- [ ]
- [ ]

Today I'm Grateful for:

Ideas/Plans

➡ = Forward   X = Delete   ✓ = Completed

Daily Breakdown:

NOTES

4 AM
5 AM
6 AM
7 AM
8 AM
9 AM
10 AM
11 AM
12 PM
1 PM
2 PM
3 PM
4 PM
5 PM
6 PM
7 PM
8 PM
9 PM
10 PM

Plan the Day to Achieve the Most Important Goals.

Thursday

Top 3 Priorities Today:
- ☐
- ☐
- ☐

Hour of Power
- ☐ Prayer / 20 min
- ☐ Read / 20 min
- ☐ Exercise / 20 min

Homework:
- ☐
- ☐
- ☐
- ☐
- ☐
- ☐

To Do:
- ☐
- ☐
- ☐
- ☐
- ☐
- ☐
- ☐
- ☐
- ☐
- ☐
- ☐
- ☐
- ☐
- ☐
- ☐
- ☐
- ☐
- ☐
- ☐
- ☐

Appointments/Dates
- ☐
- ☐
- ☐

Calls/Emails
- ☐
- ☐
- ☐
- ☐
- ☐
- ☐
- ☐

Today I'm Grateful for:

Ideas/Plans

➡ = Forward   X = Delete   ✓ = Completed

Daily Breakdown:

	NOTES

4 AM
5 AM
6 AM
7 AM
8 AM
9 AM
10 AM
11 AM
12 PM
1 PM
2 PM
3 PM
4 PM
5 PM
6 PM
7 PM
8 PM
9 PM
10 PM

Plan the Day to Achieve the Most Important Goals.		Friday
Top 3 Priorities Today: ☐ ☐ ☐	**Hour of Power** ☐ Prayer / 20 min ☐ Read / 20 min ☐ Exercise / 20 min	**Homework:** ☐ ☐ ☐ ☐ ☐ ☐
To Do: ☐		**Appointments/Dates** ☐ ☐ ☐
		Calls/Emails ☐ ☐ ☐ ☐ ☐ ☐ ☐
		Today I'm Grateful for:
Ideas/Plans		

➡ = Forward   X = Delete   ✓ = Completed

Daily Breakdown:

NOTES

4 AM
5 AM
6 AM
7 AM
8 AM
9 AM
10 AM
11 AM
12 PM
1 PM
2 PM
3 PM
4 PM
5 PM
6 PM
7 PM
8 PM
9 PM
10 PM

Weekly Reflections

How do you plan to rest this weekend?

What will you NOT do in order to find rest?

What will you do that is Life-Giving?

List 3 -5 Relationships you want to invest in this weekend:
- [ ]
- [ ]
- [ ]
- [ ]
- [ ]

How will you invest in those relationships?
- [ ]
- [ ]
- [ ]
- [ ]
- [ ]

What have I read/heard this week that stood out?

How will I implement what I learned this week?

What are my 3 Biggest Wins for this week?
- [ ]
- [ ]
- [ ]

What are my top 3 priorities for next week?
- [ ]
- [ ]
- [ ]

What God has told me to do this year:	What God did for me this week:

What God is saying Now!

What am I asking God for this week?	My next Steps to obey what God has said:

Plan the Day to Achieve the Most Important Goals.

Saturday

Top 3 Priorities Today:
- [ ]
- [ ]
- [ ]

Hour of Power
- [ ] Prayer / 20 min
- [ ] Read / 20 min
- [ ] Exercise / 20 min

Homework:
- [ ]
- [ ]
- [ ]
- [ ]
- [ ]
- [ ]

To Do:
- [ ]
- [ ]
- [ ]
- [ ]
- [ ]
- [ ]
- [ ]
- [ ]
- [ ]
- [ ]
- [ ]
- [ ]
- [ ]
- [ ]
- [ ]
- [ ]
- [ ]
- [ ]
- [ ]
- [ ]
- [ ]
- [ ]
- [ ]

Appointments/Dates
- [ ]
- [ ]
- [ ]

Calls/Emails
- [ ]
- [ ]
- [ ]
- [ ]
- [ ]
- [ ]
- [ ]

Today I'm Grateful for:

Ideas/Plans

➡ = Forward   X = Delete   ✓ = Completed

Daily Breakdown:

NOTES

4 AM
5 AM
6 AM
7 AM
8 AM
9 AM
10 AM
11 AM
12 PM
1 PM
2 PM
3 PM
4 PM
5 PM
6 PM
7 PM
8 PM
9 PM
10 PM

Plan the Day to Achieve the Most Important Goals.

Sunday

Top 3 Priorities Today:
- [ ]
- [ ]
- [ ]

Hour of Power
- [ ] Prayer / 20 min
- [ ] Read / 20 min
- [ ] Exercise / 20 min

Homework:
- [ ]
- [ ]
- [ ]
- [ ]
- [ ]
- [ ]

To Do:
- [ ]
- [ ]
- [ ]
- [ ]
- [ ]
- [ ]
- [ ]
- [ ]
- [ ]
- [ ]
- [ ]
- [ ]
- [ ]
- [ ]
- [ ]
- [ ]
- [ ]
- [ ]
- [ ]
- [ ]
- [ ]
- [ ]

Appointments/Dates
- [ ]
- [ ]
- [ ]

Calls/Emails
- [ ]
- [ ]
- [ ]
- [ ]
- [ ]
- [ ]
- [ ]

Today I'm Grateful for:

Ideas/Plans

➡ = Forward   X = Delete   ✓ = Completed

Daily Breakdown:

NOTES

4 AM
5 AM
6 AM
7 AM
8 AM
9 AM
10 AM
11 AM
12 PM
1 PM
2 PM
3 PM
4 PM
5 PM
6 PM
7 PM
8 PM
9 PM
10 PM

Weekly Time Map

Top 3 priorities this week:

Time		Monday	Tuesday	Wednesday
4 a.m.	:00			
	:30			
5 a.m.	:00			
	:30			
6 a.m.	:00			
	:30			
7 a.m.	:00			
	:30			
8 a.m.	:00			
	:30			
9 a.m.	:00			
	:30			
10 a.m.	:00			
	:30			
11 a.m.	:00			
	:30			
12 p.m.	:00			
	:30			
1 p.m.	:00			
	:30			
2 p.m.	:00			
	:30			
3 p.m.	:00			
	:30			
4 p.m.	:00			
	:30			
5 p.m.	:00			
	:30			
6 p.m.	:00			
	:30			
7 p.m.	:00			
	:30			
8 p.m.	:00			
	:30			
9 p.m.	:00			
	:30			
10 p.m.	:00			
	:30			

☐ Thursday	☐ Friday	☐ Saturday	☐ Sunday

Plan the Day to Achieve the Most Important Goals.	Monday

Top 3 Priorities Today:	Hour of Power	Homework:
☐ ☐ ☐	☐ Prayer / 20 min ☐ Read / 20 min ☐ Exercise / 20 min	☐ ☐ ☐ ☐ ☐ ☐

To Do:
☐
☐
☐
☐
☐
☐
☐
☐
☐
☐
☐
☐
☐
☐
☐
☐
☐
☐
☐
☐

Appointments/Dates
☐
☐
☐

Calls/Emails
☐
☐
☐
☐
☐
☐
☐

Today I'm Grateful for:

Ideas/Plans

➡ = Forward   X = Delete   ✓ = Completed

Daily Breakdown:

NOTES

4 AM
5 AM
6 AM
7 AM
8 AM
9 AM
10 AM
11 AM
12 PM
1 PM
2 PM
3 PM
4 PM
5 PM
6 PM
7 PM
8 PM
9 PM
10 PM

Plan the Day to Achieve the Most Important Goals.

Tuesday

Top 3 Priorities Today:
- [ ]
- [ ]
- [ ]

Hour of Power
- [ ] Prayer / 20 min
- [ ] Read / 20 min
- [ ] Exercise / 20 min

Homework:
- [ ]
- [ ]
- [ ]
- [ ]
- [ ]
- [ ]

To Do:
- [ ]
- [ ]
- [ ]
- [ ]
- [ ]
- [ ]
- [ ]
- [ ]
- [ ]
- [ ]
- [ ]
- [ ]
- [ ]
- [ ]
- [ ]
- [ ]
- [ ]
- [ ]
- [ ]
- [ ]
- [ ]

Appointments/Dates
- [ ]
- [ ]
- [ ]

Calls/Emails
- [ ]
- [ ]
- [ ]
- [ ]
- [ ]
- [ ]
- [ ]

Today I'm Grateful for:

Ideas/Plans

➡ = Forward   X = Delete   ✓ = Completed

Daily Breakdown:

NOTES

4 AM
5 AM
6 AM
7 AM
8 AM
9 AM
10 AM
11 AM
12 PM
1 PM
2 PM
3 PM
4 PM
5 PM
6 PM
7 PM
8 PM
9 PM
10 PM

Plan the Day to Achieve the Most Important Goals.

Wednesday

Top 3 Priorities Today:
- [ ]
- [ ]
- [ ]

Hour of Power
- [ ] Prayer / 20 min
- [ ] Read / 20 min
- [ ] Exercise / 20 min

Homework:
- [ ]
- [ ]
- [ ]
- [ ]
- [ ]
- [ ]

To Do:
- [ ]
- [ ]
- [ ]
- [ ]
- [ ]
- [ ]
- [ ]
- [ ]
- [ ]
- [ ]
- [ ]
- [ ]
- [ ]
- [ ]
- [ ]
- [ ]
- [ ]
- [ ]
- [ ]
- [ ]
- [ ]
- [ ]

Appointments/Dates
- [ ]
- [ ]
- [ ]

Calls/Emails
- [ ]
- [ ]
- [ ]
- [ ]
- [ ]
- [ ]
- [ ]

Today I'm Grateful for:

Ideas/Plans

➡ = Forward   X = Delete   ✓ = Completed

Daily Breakdown:

NOTES

4 AM

5 AM

6 AM

7 AM

8 AM

9 AM

10 AM

11 AM

12 PM

1 PM

2 PM

3 PM

4 PM

5 PM

6 PM

7 PM

8 PM

9 PM

10 PM

Plan the Day to Achieve the Most Important Goals.

Thursday

Top 3 Priorities Today:
- [ ]
- [ ]
- [ ]

Hour of Power
- [ ] Prayer / 20 min
- [ ] Read / 20 min
- [ ] Exercise / 20 min

Homework:
- [ ]
- [ ]
- [ ]
- [ ]
- [ ]
- [ ]

To Do:
- [ ]
- [ ]
- [ ]
- [ ]
- [ ]
- [ ]
- [ ]
- [ ]
- [ ]
- [ ]
- [ ]
- [ ]
- [ ]
- [ ]
- [ ]
- [ ]
- [ ]
- [ ]
- [ ]
- [ ]

Appointments/Dates
- [ ]
- [ ]
- [ ]

Calls/Emails
- [ ]
- [ ]
- [ ]
- [ ]
- [ ]
- [ ]
- [ ]

Today I'm Grateful for:

Ideas/Plans

➡ = Forward   X = Delete   ✓ = Completed

Daily Breakdown:

NOTES

4 AM
5 AM
6 AM
7 AM
8 AM
9 AM
10 AM
11 AM
12 PM
1 PM
2 PM
3 PM
4 PM
5 PM
6 PM
7 PM
8 PM
9 PM
10 PM

Plan the Day to Achieve the Most Important Goals.

Friday

Top 3 Priorities Today:
- [ ]
- [ ]
- [ ]

Hour of Power
- [ ] Prayer / 20 min
- [ ] Read / 20 min
- [ ] Exercise / 20 min

Homework:
- [ ]
- [ ]
- [ ]
- [ ]
- [ ]
- [ ]

To Do:
- [ ]
- [ ]
- [ ]
- [ ]
- [ ]
- [ ]
- [ ]
- [ ]
- [ ]
- [ ]
- [ ]
- [ ]
- [ ]
- [ ]
- [ ]
- [ ]
- [ ]
- [ ]
- [ ]
- [ ]
- [ ]

Appointments/Dates
- [ ]
- [ ]
- [ ]

Calls/Emails
- [ ]
- [ ]
- [ ]
- [ ]
- [ ]
- [ ]
- [ ]

Today I'm Grateful for:

Ideas/Plans

➡ = Forward   X = Delete   ✓ = Completed

Daily Breakdown:

NOTES

4 AM
5 AM
6 AM
7 AM
8 AM
9 AM
10 AM
11 AM
12 PM
1 PM
2 PM
3 PM
4 PM
5 PM
6 PM
7 PM
8 PM
9 PM
10 PM

Weekly Reflections

How do you plan to rest this weekend?

What will you NOT do in order to find rest?

What will you do that is Life-Giving?

List 3 -5 Relationships you want to invest in this weekend:
- ☐
- ☐
- ☐
- ☐
- ☐

How will you invest in those relationships?
- ☐
- ☐
- ☐
- ☐
- ☐

What have I read/heard this week that stood out?

How will I implement what I learned this week?

What are my 3 Biggest Wins for this week?
- ☐
- ☐
- ☐

What are my top 3 priorities for next week?
- ☐
- ☐
- ☐

What God has told me to do this year:	What God did for me this week:

What God is saying Now!

What am I asking God for this week?	My next Steps to obey what God has said:

Plan the Day to Achieve the Most Important Goals.

Saturday

Top 3 Priorities Today:
- [ ]
- [ ]
- [ ]

Hour of Power
- [ ] Prayer / 20 min
- [ ] Read / 20 min
- [ ] Exercise / 20 min

Homework:
- [ ]
- [ ]
- [ ]
- [ ]
- [ ]

To Do:
- [ ]
- [ ]
- [ ]
- [ ]
- [ ]
- [ ]
- [ ]
- [ ]
- [ ]
- [ ]
- [ ]
- [ ]
- [ ]
- [ ]
- [ ]
- [ ]
- [ ]
- [ ]
- [ ]
- [ ]

Appointments/Dates
- [ ]
- [ ]
- [ ]

Calls/Emails
- [ ]
- [ ]
- [ ]
- [ ]
- [ ]
- [ ]
- [ ]

Today I'm Grateful for:

Ideas/Plans

➡ = Forward   X = Delete   ✓ = Completed

Daily Breakdown:

4 AM	
5 AM	
6 AM	
7 AM	
8 AM	
9 AM	
10 AM	
11 AM	
12 PM	
1 PM	
2 PM	
3 PM	
4 PM	
5 PM	
6 PM	
7 PM	
8 PM	
9 PM	
10 PM	

NOTES

Plan the Day to Achieve the Most Important Goals.

Sunday

Top 3 Priorities Today:
- [ ]
- [ ]
- [ ]

Hour of Power
- [ ] Prayer / 20 min
- [ ] Read / 20 min
- [ ] Exercise / 20 min

Homework:
- [ ]
- [ ]
- [ ]
- [ ]
- [ ]
- [ ]

To Do:
- [ ]
- [ ]
- [ ]
- [ ]
- [ ]
- [ ]
- [ ]
- [ ]
- [ ]
- [ ]
- [ ]
- [ ]
- [ ]
- [ ]
- [ ]
- [ ]
- [ ]
- [ ]
- [ ]
- [ ]

Appointments/Dates
- [ ]
- [ ]
- [ ]

Calls/Emails
- [ ]
- [ ]
- [ ]
- [ ]
- [ ]
- [ ]
- [ ]

Today I'm Grateful for:

Ideas/Plans

➡ = Forward   X = Delete   ✓ = Completed

Daily Breakdown:

4 AM	
5 AM	
6 AM	
7 AM	
8 AM	
9 AM	
10 AM	
11 AM	
12 PM	
1 PM	
2 PM	
3 PM	
4 PM	
5 PM	
6 PM	
7 PM	
8 PM	
9 PM	
10 PM	

NOTES

Weekly Time Map

Top 3 priorities this week:

Time		Monday	Tuesday	Wednesday
4 a.m.	:00			
	:30			
5 a.m.	:00			
	:30			
6 a.m.	:00			
	:30			
7 a.m.	:00			
	:30			
8 a.m.	:00			
	:30			
9 a.m.	:00			
	:30			
10 a.m.	:00			
	:30			
11 a.m.	:00			
	:30			
12 p.m.	:00			
	:30			
1 p.m.	:00			
	:30			
2 p.m.	:00			
	:30			
3 p.m.	:00			
	:30			
4 p.m.	:00			
	:30			
5 p.m.	:00			
	:30			
6 p.m.	:00			
	:30			
7 p.m.	:00			
	:30			
8 p.m.	:00			
	:30			
9 p.m.	:00			
	:30			
10 p.m.	:00			
	:30			

Thursday	Friday	Saturday	Sunday

Plan the Day to Achieve the Most Important Goals.		Monday
Top 3 Priorities Today: ☐ ☐ ☐	Hour of Power ☐ Prayer / 20 min ☐ Read / 20 min ☐ Exercise / 20 min	Homework: ☐ ☐ ☐ ☐ ☐
To Do: ☐		Appointments/Dates ☐ ☐ ☐
^		Calls/Emails ☐ ☐ ☐ ☐ ☐ ☐ ☐
^		Today I'm Grateful for:
Ideas/Plans		^

➡ = Forward   X = Delete   ✓ = Completed

Daily Breakdown:

NOTES

4 AM
5 AM
6 AM
7 AM
8 AM
9 AM
10 AM
11 AM
12 PM
1 PM
2 PM
3 PM
4 PM
5 PM
6 PM
7 PM
8 PM
9 PM
10 PM

Plan the Day to Achieve the Most Important Goals.

Tuesday

Top 3 Priorities Today:
- [ ]
- [ ]
- [ ]

Hour of Power
- [ ] Prayer / 20 min
- [ ] Read / 20 min
- [ ] Exercise / 20 min

Homework:
- [ ]
- [ ]
- [ ]
- [ ]
- [ ]
- [ ]

To Do:
- [ ]
- [ ]
- [ ]
- [ ]
- [ ]
- [ ]
- [ ]
- [ ]
- [ ]
- [ ]
- [ ]
- [ ]
- [ ]
- [ ]
- [ ]
- [ ]
- [ ]
- [ ]
- [ ]
- [ ]
- [ ]

Appointments/Dates
- [ ]
- [ ]
- [ ]

Calls/Emails
- [ ]
- [ ]
- [ ]
- [ ]
- [ ]
- [ ]
- [ ]

Today I'm Grateful for:

Ideas/Plans

➡ = Forward   X = Delete   ✓ = Completed

Daily Breakdown:

4 AM	
5 AM	
6 AM	
7 AM	
8 AM	
9 AM	
10 AM	
11 AM	
12 PM	
1 PM	
2 PM	
3 PM	
4 PM	
5 PM	
6 PM	
7 PM	
8 PM	
9 PM	
10 PM	

NOTES

	Plan the Day to Achieve the Most Important Goals.	Wednesday

Top 3 Priorities Today:	Hour of Power	Homework:
☐	☐ Prayer / 20 min	☐
☐	☐ Read / 20 min	☐
☐	☐ Exercise / 20 min	☐

To Do:
☐
☐
☐
☐
☐
☐
☐
☐
☐
☐
☐
☐
☐
☐
☐
☐
☐
☐
☐

Appointments/Dates
☐
☐
☐

Calls/Emails
☐
☐
☐
☐
☐
☐
☐

Today I'm Grateful for:

Ideas/Plans

➡ = Forward   X = Delete   ✓ = Completed

Daily Breakdown:

NOTES

4 AM
5 AM
6 AM
7 AM
8 AM
9 AM
10 AM
11 AM
12 PM
1 PM
2 PM
3 PM
4 PM
5 PM
6 PM
7 PM
8 PM
9 PM
10 PM

Plan the Day to Achieve the Most Important Goals.	Thursday

Top 3 Priorities Today:
- [ ]
- [ ]
- [ ]

Hour of Power
- [ ] Prayer / 20 min
- [ ] Read / 20 min
- [ ] Exercise / 20 min

Homework:
- [ ]
- [ ]
- [ ]
- [ ]
- [ ]
- [ ]

To Do:
- [ ]
- [ ]
- [ ]
- [ ]
- [ ]
- [ ]
- [ ]
- [ ]
- [ ]
- [ ]
- [ ]
- [ ]
- [ ]
- [ ]
- [ ]
- [ ]
- [ ]
- [ ]
- [ ]
- [ ]
- [ ]

Appointments/Dates
- [ ]
- [ ]
- [ ]

Calls/Emails
- [ ]
- [ ]
- [ ]
- [ ]
- [ ]
- [ ]
- [ ]

Today I'm Grateful for:

Ideas/Plans

➡ = Forward   X = Delete   ✓ = Completed

Daily Breakdown:

NOTES

4 AM
5 AM
6 AM
7 AM
8 AM
9 AM
10 AM
11 AM
12 PM
1 PM
2 PM
3 PM
4 PM
5 PM
6 PM
7 PM
8 PM
9 PM
10 PM

Plan the Day to Achieve the Most Important Goals.

Friday

Top 3 Priorities Today:
- [ ]
- [ ]
- [ ]

Hour of Power
- [ ] Prayer / 20 min
- [ ] Read / 20 min
- [ ] Exercise / 20 min

Homework:
- [ ]
- [ ]
- [ ]
- [ ]
- [ ]
- [ ]

To Do:
- [ ]
- [ ]
- [ ]
- [ ]
- [ ]
- [ ]
- [ ]
- [ ]
- [ ]
- [ ]
- [ ]
- [ ]
- [ ]
- [ ]
- [ ]
- [ ]
- [ ]
- [ ]
- [ ]
- [ ]
- [ ]

Appointments/Dates
- [ ]
- [ ]
- [ ]

Calls/Emails
- [ ]
- [ ]
- [ ]
- [ ]
- [ ]
- [ ]
- [ ]

Today I'm Grateful for:

Ideas/Plans

➡ = Forward   X = Delete   ✓ = Completed

Daily Breakdown:

4 AM
5 AM
6 AM
7 AM
8 AM
9 AM
10 AM
11 AM
12 PM
1 PM
2 PM
3 PM
4 PM
5 PM
6 PM
7 PM
8 PM
9 PM
10 PM

NOTES

Weekly Reflections

How do you plan to rest this weekend?

What will you NOT do in order to find rest?

What will you do that is Life-Giving?

List 3-5 Relationships you want to invest in this weekend:
- ☐
- ☐
- ☐
- ☐
- ☐

How will you invest in those relationships?
- ☐
- ☐
- ☐
- ☐
- ☐

What have I read/heard this week that stood out?

How will I implement what I learned this week?

What are my 3 Biggest Wins for this week?
- ☐
- ☐
- ☐

What are my top 3 priorities for next week?
- ☐
- ☐
- ☐

What God has told me to do this year:	What God did for me this week:

What God is saying Now!

What am I asking God for this week?	My next Steps to obey what God has said:

Plan the Day to Achieve the Most Important Goals.

Saturday

Top 3 Priorities Today:
- ☐
- ☐
- ☐

Hour of Power
- ☐ Prayer / 20 min
- ☐ Read / 20 min
- ☐ Exercise / 20 min

Homework:
- ☐
- ☐
- ☐
- ☐
- ☐
- ☐

To Do:
- ☐
- ☐
- ☐
- ☐
- ☐
- ☐
- ☐
- ☐
- ☐
- ☐
- ☐
- ☐
- ☐
- ☐
- ☐
- ☐
- ☐
- ☐
- ☐
- ☐
- ☐

Appointments/Dates
- ☐
- ☐
- ☐

Calls/Emails
- ☐
- ☐
- ☐
- ☐
- ☐
- ☐
- ☐

Today I'm Grateful for:

Ideas/Plans

➡ = Forward   X = Delete   ✓ = Completed

Daily Breakdown:

NOTES

4 AM
5 AM
6 AM
7 AM
8 AM
9 AM
10 AM
11 AM
12 PM
1 PM
2 PM
3 PM
4 PM
5 PM
6 PM
7 PM
8 PM
9 PM
10 PM

Plan the Day to Achieve the Most Important Goals.

Sunday

Top 3 Priorities Today:
- [ ]
- [ ]
- [ ]

Hour of Power
- [ ] Prayer / 20 min
- [ ] Read / 20 min
- [ ] Exercise / 20 min

Homework:
- [ ]
- [ ]
- [ ]
- [ ]
- [ ]
- [ ]

To Do:
- [ ]
- [ ]
- [ ]
- [ ]
- [ ]
- [ ]
- [ ]
- [ ]
- [ ]
- [ ]
- [ ]
- [ ]
- [ ]
- [ ]
- [ ]
- [ ]
- [ ]
- [ ]
- [ ]
- [ ]

Appointments/Dates
- [ ]
- [ ]
- [ ]

Calls/Emails
- [ ]
- [ ]
- [ ]
- [ ]
- [ ]
- [ ]
- [ ]

Today I'm Grateful for:

Ideas/Plans

➡ = Forward   X = Delete   ✓ = Completed

Daily Breakdown:

4 AM	
5 AM	
6 AM	
7 AM	
8 AM	
9 AM	
10 AM	
11 AM	
12 PM	
1 PM	
2 PM	
3 PM	
4 PM	
5 PM	
6 PM	
7 PM	
8 PM	
9 PM	
10 PM	

NOTES

Weekly Time Map

Top 3 priorities this week:

Time		Monday	Tuesday	Wednesday
4 a.m.	:00			
	:30			
5 a.m.	:00			
	:30			
6 a.m.	:00			
	:30			
7 a.m.	:00			
	:30			
8 a.m.	:00			
	:30			
9 a.m.	:00			
	:30			
10 a.m.	:00			
	:30			
11 a.m.	:00			
	:30			
12 p.m.	:00			
	:30			
1 p.m.	:00			
	:30			
2 p.m.	:00			
	:30			
3 p.m.	:00			
	:30			
4 p.m.	:00			
	:30			
5 p.m.	:00			
	:30			
6 p.m.	:00			
	:30			
7 p.m.	:00			
	:30			
8 p.m.	:00			
	:30			
9 p.m.	:00			
	:30			
10 p.m.	:00			
	:30			

Thursday	Friday	Saturday	Sunday

Plan the Day to Achieve the Most Important Goals.

Monday

Top 3 Priorities Today:
- ☐
- ☐
- ☐

Hour of Power
- ☐ Prayer / 20 min
- ☐ Read / 20 min
- ☐ Exercise / 20 min

Homework:
- ☐
- ☐
- ☐
- ☐
- ☐

To Do:
- ☐
- ☐
- ☐
- ☐
- ☐
- ☐
- ☐
- ☐
- ☐
- ☐
- ☐
- ☐
- ☐
- ☐
- ☐
- ☐
- ☐
- ☐
- ☐
- ☐

Appointments/Dates
- ☐
- ☐
- ☐

Calls/Emails
- ☐
- ☐
- ☐
- ☐
- ☐
- ☐
- ☐

Today I'm Grateful for:

Ideas/Plans

➡ = Forward   X = Delete   ✓ = Completed

Daily Breakdown:

NOTES

4 AM
5 AM
6 AM
7 AM
8 AM
9 AM
10 AM
11 AM
12 PM
1 PM
2 PM
3 PM
4 PM
5 PM
6 PM
7 PM
8 PM
9 PM
10 PM

Plan the Day to Achieve the Most Important Goals.

Tuesday

Top 3 Priorities Today:
- [ ]
- [ ]
- [ ]

Hour of Power
- [ ] Prayer / 20 min
- [ ] Read / 20 min
- [ ] Exercise / 20 min

Homework:
- [ ]
- [ ]
- [ ]
- [ ]
- [ ]
- [ ]

To Do:
- [ ]
- [ ]
- [ ]
- [ ]
- [ ]
- [ ]
- [ ]
- [ ]
- [ ]
- [ ]
- [ ]
- [ ]
- [ ]
- [ ]
- [ ]
- [ ]
- [ ]
- [ ]
- [ ]
- [ ]

Appointments/Dates
- [ ]
- [ ]
- [ ]

Calls/Emails
- [ ]
- [ ]
- [ ]
- [ ]
- [ ]
- [ ]
- [ ]

Today I'm Grateful for:

Ideas/Plans

➡ = Forward   X = Delete   ✓ = Completed

Daily Breakdown:

NOTES

4 AM
5 AM
6 AM
7 AM
8 AM
9 AM
10 AM
11 AM
12 PM
1 PM
2 PM
3 PM
4 PM
5 PM
6 PM
7 PM
8 PM
9 PM
10 PM

Plan the Day to Achieve the Most Important Goals.

Wednesday

Top 3 Priorities Today:
- [ ]
- [ ]
- [ ]

Hour of Power
- [ ] Prayer / 20 min
- [ ] Read / 20 min
- [ ] Exercise / 20 min

Homework:
- [ ]
- [ ]
- [ ]
- [ ]
- [ ]
- [ ]

To Do:
- [ ]
- [ ]
- [ ]
- [ ]
- [ ]
- [ ]
- [ ]
- [ ]
- [ ]
- [ ]
- [ ]
- [ ]
- [ ]
- [ ]
- [ ]
- [ ]
- [ ]
- [ ]
- [ ]
- [ ]
- [ ]
- [ ]

Appointments/Dates
- [ ]
- [ ]
- [ ]

Calls/Emails
- [ ]
- [ ]
- [ ]
- [ ]
- [ ]
- [ ]
- [ ]

Today I'm Grateful for:

Ideas/Plans

➡ = Forward   X = Delete   ✓ = Completed

Daily Breakdown:

	NOTES

4 AM
5 AM
6 AM
7 AM
8 AM
9 AM
10 AM
11 AM
12 PM
1 PM
2 PM
3 PM
4 PM
5 PM
6 PM
7 PM
8 PM
9 PM
10 PM

Plan the Day to Achieve the Most Important Goals.

Thursday

Top 3 Priorities Today:
- ☐
- ☐
- ☐

Hour of Power
- ☐ Prayer / 20 min
- ☐ Read / 20 min
- ☐ Exercise / 20 min

Homework:
- ☐
- ☐
- ☐
- ☐
- ☐
- ☐

To Do:
- ☐
- ☐
- ☐
- ☐
- ☐
- ☐
- ☐
- ☐
- ☐
- ☐
- ☐
- ☐
- ☐
- ☐
- ☐
- ☐
- ☐
- ☐
- ☐

Appointments/Dates
- ☐
- ☐
- ☐

Calls/Emails
- ☐
- ☐
- ☐
- ☐
- ☐
- ☐
- ☐

Today I'm Grateful for:

Ideas/Plans

➡ = Forward   X = Delete   ✓ = Completed

Daily Breakdown:

NOTES

4 AM
5 AM
6 AM
7 AM
8 AM
9 AM
10 AM
11 AM
12 PM
1 PM
2 PM
3 PM
4 PM
5 PM
6 PM
7 PM
8 PM
9 PM
10 PM

Plan the Day to Achieve the Most Important Goals.

Friday

Top 3 Priorities Today:
- [ ]
- [ ]
- [ ]

Hour of Power
- [ ] Prayer / 20 min
- [ ] Read / 20 min
- [ ] Exercise / 20 min

Homework:
- [ ]
- [ ]
- [ ]
- [ ]
- [ ]
- [ ]

To Do:
- [ ]
- [ ]
- [ ]
- [ ]
- [ ]
- [ ]
- [ ]
- [ ]
- [ ]
- [ ]
- [ ]
- [ ]
- [ ]
- [ ]
- [ ]
- [ ]
- [ ]
- [ ]
- [ ]
- [ ]

Appointments/Dates
- [ ]
- [ ]
- [ ]

Calls/Emails
- [ ]
- [ ]
- [ ]
- [ ]
- [ ]
- [ ]
- [ ]

Today I'm Grateful for:

Ideas/Plans

➡ = Forward   X = Delete   ✓ = Completed

Daily Breakdown:

NOTES

4 AM
5 AM
6 AM
7 AM
8 AM
9 AM
10 AM
11 AM
12 PM
1 PM
2 PM
3 PM
4 PM
5 PM
6 PM
7 PM
8 PM
9 PM
10 PM

Weekly Reflections

How do you plan to rest this weekend?

What will you NOT do in order to find rest?

What will you do that is Life-Giving?

List 3 -5 Relationships you want to invest in this weekend:
- [ ]
- [ ]
- [ ]
- [ ]
- [ ]

How will you invest in those relationships?
- [ ]
- [ ]
- [ ]
- [ ]
- [ ]

What have I read/heard this week that stood out?

How will I implement what I learned this week?

What are my 3 Biggest Wins for this week?
- [ ]
- [ ]
- [ ]

What are my top 3 priorities for next week?
- [ ]
- [ ]
- [ ]

| What God has told me to do this year: | What God did for me this week: |

What God is saying Now!

| What am I asking God for this week? | My next Steps to obey what God has said: |

Plan the Day to Achieve the Most Important Goals.

Saturday

Top 3 Priorities Today:
- [ ]
- [ ]
- [ ]

Hour of Power
- [ ] Prayer / 20 min
- [ ] Read / 20 min
- [ ] Exercise / 20 min

Homework:
- [ ]
- [ ]
- [ ]
- [ ]
- [ ]
- [ ]

To Do:
- [ ]
- [ ]
- [ ]
- [ ]
- [ ]
- [ ]
- [ ]
- [ ]
- [ ]
- [ ]
- [ ]
- [ ]
- [ ]
- [ ]
- [ ]
- [ ]
- [ ]
- [ ]
- [ ]
- [ ]
- [ ]

Appointments/Dates
- [ ]
- [ ]
- [ ]

Calls/Emails
- [ ]
- [ ]
- [ ]
- [ ]
- [ ]
- [ ]
- [ ]

Today I'm Grateful for:

Ideas/Plans

➡ = Forward   X = Delete   ✓ = Completed

Daily Breakdown:

NOTES

4 AM
5 AM
6 AM
7 AM
8 AM
9 AM
10 AM
11 AM
12 PM
1 PM
2 PM
3 PM
4 PM
5 PM
6 PM
7 PM
8 PM
9 PM
10 PM

Plan the Day to Achieve the Most Important Goals.

Sunday

Top 3 Priorities Today:
- [ ]
- [ ]
- [ ]

Hour of Power
- [ ] Prayer / 20 min
- [ ] Read / 20 min
- [ ] Exercise / 20 min

Homework:
- [ ]
- [ ]
- [ ]
- [ ]
- [ ]
- [ ]

To Do:
- [ ]
- [ ]
- [ ]
- [ ]
- [ ]
- [ ]
- [ ]
- [ ]
- [ ]
- [ ]
- [ ]
- [ ]
- [ ]
- [ ]
- [ ]
- [ ]
- [ ]
- [ ]
- [ ]
- [ ]
- [ ]
- [ ]

Appointments/Dates
- [ ]
- [ ]
- [ ]

Calls/Emails
- [ ]
- [ ]
- [ ]
- [ ]
- [ ]
- [ ]
- [ ]

Today I'm Grateful for:

Ideas/Plans

➡ = Forward   X = Delete   ✓ = Completed

Daily Breakdown:

Time	
4 AM	
5 AM	
6 AM	
7 AM	
8 AM	
9 AM	
10 AM	
11 AM	
12 PM	
1 PM	
2 PM	
3 PM	
4 PM	
5 PM	
6 PM	
7 PM	
8 PM	
9 PM	
10 PM	

NOTES

Weekly Time Map

Top 3 priorities this week:

Time		Monday	Tuesday	Wednesday
4 a.m.	:00			
	:30			
5 a.m.	:00			
	:30			
6 a.m.	:00			
	:30			
7 a.m.	:00			
	:30			
8 a.m.	:00			
	:30			
9 a.m.	:00			
	:30			
10 a.m.	:00			
	:30			
11 a.m.	:00			
	:30			
12 p.m.	:00			
	:30			
1 p.m.	:00			
	:30			
2 p.m.	:00			
	:30			
3 p.m.	:00			
	:30			
4 p.m.	:00			
	:30			
5 p.m.	:00			
	:30			
6 p.m.	:00			
	:30			
7 p.m.	:00			
	:30			
8 p.m.	:00			
	:30			
9 p.m.	:00			
	:30			
10 p.m.	:00			
	:30			

☐ Thursday	☐ Friday	☐ Saturday	☐ Sunday

Plan the Day to Achieve the Most Important Goals.

Monday

Top 3 Priorities Today:
- [ ]
- [ ]
- [ ]

Hour of Power
- [ ] Prayer / 20 min
- [ ] Read / 20 min
- [ ] Exercise / 20 min

Homework:
- [ ]
- [ ]
- [ ]
- [ ]
- [ ]
- [ ]

To Do:
- [ ]
- [ ]
- [ ]
- [ ]
- [ ]
- [ ]
- [ ]
- [ ]
- [ ]
- [ ]
- [ ]
- [ ]
- [ ]
- [ ]
- [ ]
- [ ]
- [ ]
- [ ]
- [ ]
- [ ]
- [ ]

Appointments/Dates
- [ ]
- [ ]
- [ ]

Calls/Emails
- [ ]
- [ ]
- [ ]
- [ ]
- [ ]
- [ ]
- [ ]

Today I'm Grateful for:

Ideas/Plans

➡ = Forward   X = Delete   ✓ = Completed

Daily Breakdown:

	NOTES

4 AM
5 AM
6 AM
7 AM
8 AM
9 AM
10 AM
11 AM
12 PM
1 PM
2 PM
3 PM
4 PM
5 PM
6 PM
7 PM
8 PM
9 PM
10 PM

Plan the Day to Achieve the Most Important Goals.

Tuesday

Top 3 Priorities Today:
- [ ]
- [ ]
- [ ]

Hour of Power
- [ ] Prayer / 20 min
- [ ] Read / 20 min
- [ ] Exercise / 20 min

Homework:
- [ ]
- [ ]
- [ ]
- [ ]
- [ ]
- [ ]

To Do:
- [ ]
- [ ]
- [ ]
- [ ]
- [ ]
- [ ]
- [ ]
- [ ]
- [ ]
- [ ]
- [ ]
- [ ]
- [ ]
- [ ]
- [ ]
- [ ]
- [ ]
- [ ]
- [ ]
- [ ]

Appointments/Dates
- [ ]
- [ ]
- [ ]

Calls/Emails
- [ ]
- [ ]
- [ ]
- [ ]
- [ ]
- [ ]
- [ ]

Today I'm Grateful for:

Ideas/Plans

➡ = Forward   X = Delete   ✓ = Completed

Daily Breakdown:

NOTES

4 AM
5 AM
6 AM
7 AM
8 AM
9 AM
10 AM
11 AM
12 PM
1 PM
2 PM
3 PM
4 PM
5 PM
6 PM
7 PM
8 PM
9 PM
10 PM

Plan the Day to Achieve the Most Important Goals.

Wednesday

Top 3 Priorities Today:
- [ ]
- [ ]
- [ ]

Hour of Power
- [ ] Prayer / 20 min
- [ ] Read / 20 min
- [ ] Exercise / 20 min

Homework:
- [ ]
- [ ]
- [ ]
- [ ]
- [ ]
- [ ]

To Do:
- [ ]
- [ ]
- [ ]
- [ ]
- [ ]
- [ ]
- [ ]
- [ ]
- [ ]
- [ ]
- [ ]
- [ ]
- [ ]
- [ ]
- [ ]
- [ ]
- [ ]
- [ ]
- [ ]
- [ ]
- [ ]

Appointments/Dates
- [ ]
- [ ]
- [ ]

Calls/Emails
- [ ]
- [ ]
- [ ]
- [ ]
- [ ]
- [ ]
- [ ]

Today I'm Grateful for:

Ideas/Plans

➡ = Forward   X = Delete   ✓ = Completed

Daily Breakdown:

NOTES

4 AM
5 AM
6 AM
7 AM
8 AM
9 AM
10 AM
11 AM
12 PM
1 PM
2 PM
3 PM
4 PM
5 PM
6 PM
7 PM
8 PM
9 PM
10 PM

Plan the Day to Achieve the Most Important Goals.

Thursday

Top 3 Priorities Today:
- [ ]
- [ ]
- [ ]

Hour of Power
- [ ] Prayer / 20 min
- [ ] Read / 20 min
- [ ] Exercise / 20 min

Homework:
- [ ]
- [ ]
- [ ]
- [ ]
- [ ]
- [ ]

To Do:
- [ ]
- [ ]
- [ ]
- [ ]
- [ ]
- [ ]
- [ ]
- [ ]
- [ ]
- [ ]
- [ ]
- [ ]
- [ ]
- [ ]
- [ ]
- [ ]
- [ ]
- [ ]
- [ ]
- [ ]
- [ ]

Appointments/Dates
- [ ]
- [ ]
- [ ]

Calls/Emails
- [ ]
- [ ]
- [ ]
- [ ]
- [ ]
- [ ]
- [ ]

Today I'm Grateful for:

Ideas/Plans

➡ = Forward   X = Delete   ✓ = Completed

Daily Breakdown:

4 AM	
5 AM	
6 AM	
7 AM	
8 AM	
9 AM	
10 AM	
11 AM	
12 PM	
1 PM	
2 PM	
3 PM	
4 PM	
5 PM	
6 PM	
7 PM	
8 PM	
9 PM	
10 PM	

NOTES

Plan the Day to Achieve the Most Important Goals.

Friday

Top 3 Priorities Today:
- [ ]
- [ ]
- [ ]

Hour of Power
- [ ] Prayer / 20 min
- [ ] Read / 20 min
- [ ] Exercise / 20 min

Homework:
- [ ]
- [ ]
- [ ]
- [ ]
- [ ]
- [ ]

To Do:
- [ ]
- [ ]
- [ ]
- [ ]
- [ ]
- [ ]
- [ ]
- [ ]
- [ ]
- [ ]
- [ ]
- [ ]
- [ ]
- [ ]
- [ ]
- [ ]
- [ ]
- [ ]
- [ ]

Appointments/Dates
- [ ]
- [ ]
- [ ]

Calls/Emails
- [ ]
- [ ]
- [ ]
- [ ]
- [ ]
- [ ]
- [ ]

Today I'm Grateful for:

Ideas/Plans

➡ = Forward   X = Delete   ✓ = Completed

Daily Breakdown:

NOTES

- 4 AM
- 5 AM
- 6 AM
- 7 AM
- 8 AM
- 9 AM
- 10 AM
- 11 AM
- 12 PM
- 1 PM
- 2 PM
- 3 PM
- 4 PM
- 5 PM
- 6 PM
- 7 PM
- 8 PM
- 9 PM
- 10 PM

Weekly Reflections

How do you plan to rest this weekend?

What will you NOT do in order to find rest?

What will you do that is Life-Giving?

List 3 -5 Relationships you want to invest in this weekend:
- [ ]
- [ ]
- [ ]
- [ ]
- [ ]

How will you invest in those relationships?
- [ ]
- [ ]
- [ ]
- [ ]
- [ ]

What have I read/heard this week that stood out?

How will I implement what I learned this week?

What are my 3 Biggest Wins for this week?
- [ ]
- [ ]
- [ ]

What are my top 3 priorities for next week?
- [ ]
- [ ]
- [ ]

What God has told me to do this year:	What God did for me this week:

What God is saying Now!

What am I asking God for this week?	My next Steps to obey what God has said:

Plan the Day to Achieve the Most Important Goals.

Saturday

Top 3 Priorities Today:
- [ ]
- [ ]
- [ ]

Hour of Power
- [ ] Prayer / 20 min
- [ ] Read / 20 min
- [ ] Exercise / 20 min

Homework:
- [ ]
- [ ]
- [ ]
- [ ]
- [ ]

To Do:
- [ ]
- [ ]
- [ ]
- [ ]
- [ ]
- [ ]
- [ ]
- [ ]
- [ ]
- [ ]
- [ ]
- [ ]
- [ ]
- [ ]
- [ ]
- [ ]
- [ ]
- [ ]
- [ ]
- [ ]

Appointments/Dates
- [ ]
- [ ]
- [ ]

Calls/Emails
- [ ]
- [ ]
- [ ]
- [ ]
- [ ]
- [ ]
- [ ]

Today I'm Grateful for:

Ideas/Plans

➡ = Forward   X = Delete   ✓ = Completed

Daily Breakdown:

Time	
4 AM	
5 AM	
6 AM	
7 AM	
8 AM	
9 AM	
10 AM	
11 AM	
12 PM	
1 PM	
2 PM	
3 PM	
4 PM	
5 PM	
6 PM	
7 PM	
8 PM	
9 PM	
10 PM	

NOTES

Plan the Day to Achieve the Most Important Goals.

Sunday

Top 3 Priorities Today:
- [ ]
- [ ]
- [ ]

Hour of Power
- [ ] Prayer / 20 min
- [ ] Read / 20 min
- [ ] Exercise / 20 min

Homework:
- [ ]
- [ ]
- [ ]
- [ ]
- [ ]
- [ ]

To Do:
- [ ]
- [ ]
- [ ]
- [ ]
- [ ]
- [ ]
- [ ]
- [ ]
- [ ]
- [ ]
- [ ]
- [ ]
- [ ]
- [ ]
- [ ]
- [ ]
- [ ]
- [ ]
- [ ]
- [ ]

Appointments/Dates
- [ ]
- [ ]
- [ ]

Calls/Emails
- [ ]
- [ ]
- [ ]
- [ ]
- [ ]
- [ ]
- [ ]

Today I'm Grateful for:

Ideas/Plans

➡ = Forward   X = Delete   ✓ = Completed

Daily Breakdown:

4 AM
5 AM
6 AM
7 AM
8 AM
9 AM
10 AM
11 AM
12 PM
1 PM
2 PM
3 PM
4 PM
5 PM
6 PM
7 PM
8 PM
9 PM
10 PM

NOTES

MAIN IDEA

KEY CHANGES TO MAKE:

TIME REQUIREMENTS:

RESOURCES NEEDED:

SUPPORT/PERSONAL NEEDS:

STEPS TO EXECUTION:

| GAINS | LOSS |

IDEA

| ACTIONS OR NEXT STEPS | NOTES |

EXPLORE THE IDEA...

NOTES

NEXT STEPS

IDEA MAPPING

MAIN IDEA

KEY CHANGES TO MAKE:

TIME REQUIREMENTS:

RESOURCES NEEDED:

SUPPORT/PERSONAL NEEDS:

STEPS TO EXECUTION:

GAINS	LOSS

IDEA

ACTIONS OR NEXT STEPS	NOTES

EXPLORE THE IDEA...

NOTES

NEXT STEPS

MAIN IDEA

KEY CHANGES TO MAKE:

TIME REQUIREMENTS:

RESOURCES NEEDED:

SUPPORT/PERSONAL NEEDS:

STEPS TO EXECUTION:

GAINS	LOSS

IDEA

ACTIONS OR NEXT STEPS	NOTES

EXPLORE THE IDEA...

NOTES

NEXT STEPS

IDEA MAPPING

STUDY SUBJECT

VERSES

THOUGHTS/MEDITATION

QUOTES

Titles/Wording

1.
2.
3.
4.
5.
6.
7.
8.
9.
10.

Further Research

STUDY SUBJECT

VERSES

THOUGHTS/MEDITATION

QUOTES

Titles/Wording

1.
2.
3.
4.
5.
6.
7.
8.
9.
10.

Further Research

STUDY SUBJECT

VERSES

THOUGHTS/MEDITATION

QUOTES

Titles/Wording

1.
2.
3.
4.
5.
6.
7.
8.
9.
10.

Further Research

STUDY SUBJECT

VERSES

THOUGHTS/MEDITATION

QUOTES

Titles/Wording
1.
2.
3.
4.
5.
6.
7.
8.
9.
10.

Further Research

STUDY SUBJECT

VERSES

-
-
-
-
-
-
-
-
-
-
-
-
-
-
-
-
-
-
-
-
-
-
-
-

THOUGHTS/MEDITATION

QUOTES

Titles/Wording

1.
2.
3.
4.
5.
6.
7.
8.
9.
10.

Further Research

-
-
-
-
-
-
-
-

STUDY SUBJECT

VERSES

- [ ]
- [ ]
- [ ]
- [ ]
- [ ]
- [ ]
- [ ]
- [ ]
- [ ]
- [ ]
- [ ]
- [ ]
- [ ]
- [ ]
- [ ]
- [ ]
- [ ]
- [ ]
- [ ]
- [ ]
- [ ]
- [ ]

THOUGHTS/MEDITATION

QUOTES

Titles/Wording

1.
2.
3.
4.
5.
6.
7.
8.
9.
10.

Further Research

- [ ]
- [ ]
- [ ]
- [ ]
- [ ]
- [ ]
- [ ]
- [ ]

STUDY SUBJECT

VERSES

THOUGHTS/MEDITATION

QUOTES

Titles/Wording

1.
2.
3.
4.
5.
6.
7.
8.
9.
10.

Further Research

STUDY SUBJECT

VERSES

-
-
-
-
-
-
-
-
-
-
-
-
-
-
-
-
-
-
-
-
-
-
-
-

THOUGHTS/MEDITATION

QUOTES

Titles/Wording

1.
2.
3.
4.
5.
6.
7.
8.
9.
10.

Further Research

-
-
-
-
-
-
-
-

Books to Buy:

Audio Books to Buy:

Podcast to Download:

Books to Buy:

Audio Books to Buy:

Podcast to Download:

Books to Buy:

Audio Books to Buy:

Podcast to Download:

Books to Buy:

Audio Books to Buy:

Podcast to Download:

NOTES

NOTES

NOTES

NOTES

NOTES

NOTES

NOTES

NOTES

NOTES

NOTES

NOTES

NOTES

NOTES

NOTES

NOTES

NOTES

NOTES

NOTES

NOTES

NOTES

NOTES

NOTES

NOTES

NOTES

NOTES

NOTES

NOTES

NOTES

NOTES

NOTES

NOTES

NOTES

NOTES

NOTES

NOTES

NOTES

NOTES

NOTES

NOTES

NOTES

Ues the extra months for tracking plans coming up in the next 6 months that are not in your current quarter.

Month _____

Sun	Mon	Tues	Wed	Thurs	Fri	Sat

NOTES

Ues the extra months for tracking plans coming up in the next 6 months that are not in your current quarter.

Month _____

Sun	Mon	Tues	Wed	Thurs	Fri	Sat

NOTES

Ues the extra months for tracking plans coming up in the next 6 months that are not in your current quarter.

Month _____

Sun	Mon	Tues	Wed	Thurs	Fri	Sat

NOTES

Ues the extra months for tracking plans coming up in the next 6 months that are not in your current quarter.

Month _____

Sun	Mon	Tues	Wed	Thurs	Fri	Sat

NOTES

Ues the extra months for tracking plans coming up in the next 6 months that are not in your current quarter.

Month _____

Sun	Mon	Tues	Wed	Thurs	Fri	Sat

NOTES

Ues the extra months for tracking plans coming up in the next 6 months that are not in your current quarter.

Month _____

Sun	Mon	Tues	Wed	Thurs	Fri	Sat

NOTES

BIBLE READING CHART

I AM GOD O⎯⎯⎯⎯⎯⎯⎯⎯   *Your Name*

Old Testament

Book	Chapters
Genesis	○○○
Exodus	○○
Leviticus	○○○○○○○○○○○○○○○○○○○○○○○○○○○
Numbers	○○○○○○○○○○○○○○○○○○○○○○○○○○○○○○○○○○○
Deuteronomy	○○○○○○○○○○○○○○○○○○○○○○○○○○○○○○○○○○
Joshua	○○○○○○○○○○○○○○○○○○○○○○○○
Judges	○○○○○○○○○○○○○○○○○○○○○
Ruth	○○○○
1 Samuel	○○○○○○○○○○○○○○○○○○○○○○○○○○○○○○○
2 Samuel	○○○○○○○○○○○○○○○○○○○○○○○○
1 Kings	○○○○○○○○○○○○○○○○○○○○○○

Book	Chapters
2 Kings	○○○○○○○○○○○○○○○○○○○○○○○○○
1 Chronicles	○○○○○○○○○○○○○○○○○○○○○○○○○○○
1 Chronicles	○○○○○○○○○○○○○○○○○○○○○○○○○○○○○○○○
Ezra	○○○○○○○○○○
Nehemiah	○○○○○○○○○○○○○
Esther	○○○○○○○○○○
Job	○○
Psalms	○○○
Proverbs	○○○○○○○○○○○○○○○○○○○○○○○○○○○○○○
Ecclesiastes	○○○○○○○○○○○○
Song of Solomon	○○○○○○○○
Isaiah	○○
Jeremiah	○○○

Lamentations	○○○○○
Ezekiel	○○○
Daniel	○○○○○○○○○○○○
Hosea	○○○○○○○○○○○○○○
Joel	○○○
Amos	○○○○○○○○○
Obadiah	○
Jonah	○○○○
Micah	○○○○○○○
Nahum	○○○
Habakkuk	○○○
Zephaniah	○○○
Haggai	○○○
Zechariah	○○○○○○○○○○○○○○
Malachi	○○○○

New Testament

Matthew	○○○○○○○○○○○○○○○○○○○○○○○○○○○
Mark	○○○○○○○○○○○○○○○○
Luke	○○○○○○○○○○○○○○○○○○○○○○○○
John	○○○○○○○○○○○○○○○○○○○○○
Acts	○○○○○○○○○○○○○○○○○○○○○○○○○○○○
Romans	○○○○○○○○○○○○

1 Corinthians	○○○○○○○○○○○○○○○○
2 Corinthians	○○○○○○○○○○○○○
Galatians	○○○○○○
Ephesians	○○○○○○
Philippians	○○○○
Colossians	○○○○
1 Thessalonians	○○○○○
2 Thessalonians	○○○
1 Timothy	○○○○○○
2 Timothy	○○○○
Titus	○○○
Philemon	○
Hebrews	○○○○○○○○○○○○○
James	○○○○○
1 Peter	○○○○○
2 Peter	○○○
1 John	○○○○○
2 John	○
3 John	○
Jude	○
Revelation	○○○○○○○○○○○○○○○○○○○○○○

DATE STARTED:

DATE FINISHED: